BASIC FREUD

Also by Michael Kahn

Between Therapist and Client

The Tao of Conversation

BASIC FREUD

*Psychoanalytic Thought for
the Twenty First Century*

Michael Kahn

BASIC
BOOKS

A Member of the Perseus Books Group

Published by Basic Books,
A Member of the Perseus Books Group.

Library of Congress Cataloging-in-Publication Data
Kahn, Michael, 1924-
    Basic Freud : psychoanalytic thought for the 21st century / Michael Kahn
        p. cm
    Includes bibliographical references and index.
    ISBN 0-465-03716-X
        1. Psychoanalysis. 2. Freud, Sigmund, 1856-1939. I. Title.

BF173 .K32 2001
150.19'52—dc21

                                                                    2001043854

Design by Heather Hutchison.
Set in 11.5 pt Simoncini Garamond by the Perseus Books Group.

FIRST PAPERBACK EDITION

DHSB   05 06 07 08   15 14 13 12 11 10 9 8 7 6

For Jonathan

CONTENTS

Preface   xi
Acknowledgments   xiii

1   Introduction   1

2   The Unconscious   15

3   Psychosexual Development   35

4   The Oedipus Complex   55

5   The Repetition Compulsion   93

6   Anxiety   105

7   The Defense Mechanisms   121

8   Guilt   137

9   Dreams   155

10 Grief and Mourning   171

11 Transference   181

12 Conclusion   201

Notes   207
Bibliography   215
Index   219

The unconscious sends all sorts of vapors, odd beings, terrors, and deluding images up into the mind—whether in dream, broad daylight, or insanity; for the human kingdom, beneath the floor of the comparatively neat little dwelling that we call our consciousness, goes down into unsuspected Aladdin caves. There not only jewels but also dangerous jinn abide: the inconvenient or resisted psychological powers that we have not thought or dared to integrate into our lives. And they may remain unsuspected, or, on the other hand, some chance word, the smell of a landscape, the taste of a cup of tea, or the glance of an eye may touch a magic spring, and then dangerous messengers begin to appear in the brain. These are dangerous because they threaten the fabric of the security into which we have built ourselves and our family. But they are fiendishly fascinating too, for they carry keys that open the whole realm of the desired and feared adventure of the discovery of the self.

—Joseph Campbell,
The Hero with a Thousand Faces

PREFACE

My undergraduate years were interrupted by a world war in which I saw combat. That period was packed with a density of experience likely never to be repeated in my life. I was flooded with intense new feelings and conflicts, and the cumulative effect was bewildering. Had I been spared for a life of self-gratification or one of service? How was I to integrate the uninhibited promiscuity common to many soldiers with the expectations of marriage and family? And so on. When I returned to college I wandered into a course on Freud's theory of the unconscious and found myself in a world unlike any I had ever imagined. I was excited and intrigued. Here, I thought, was a way of dealing with my bewilderment. Here was a way of looking at feelings and conflicts that offered to make sense of them. I found the elegance and drama of the theory downright beautiful. Over the long years that I have studied this theory and taught it, it has never lost its fascination for me. During the many years that I have tried to help my clients understand themselves, I have never found another theory that so illuminates their worlds.

This book is an attempt to convey my sense of that beauty and efficacy. I intend it to cover those aspects of Freud's theory that I hope will be useful to those wanting to better understand their internal world. I believe those same aspects of the theory will be useful to clinicians wanting to better understand their clients. Therapists trained outside of specifically psychoanalytic institutes are often given only the most rudimentary introduction to Freudian theory. It seems to me they are thus deprived of indispensable tools for understanding and working with their clients. I hope this book will help remedy that.

The spirit in which I wrote this book, and the spirit in which I hope you will read it, has been nicely expressed by one of Freud's most articulate followers, Bruno Bettelheim:

> By exploring and understanding the origins and the potency of [the forces that reside in the depths of our soul] we not only become much better able to cope with them, but also gain a much deeper and more compassionate understanding of our fellow man.[1]

ACKNOWLEDGMENTS

I am very grateful to Jo Ann Miller, my editor at Basic Books. She saw in a slim proposal the possibility of a useful book. She has been a pleasure to work with, cheerful, and extremely helpful. Kay Mariea was my very cooperative project editor and Sharon DeJohn my careful and skillful copy editor.

My life partner, Virginia Kahn, put up with a great deal, including months without an available partner in her social life. Her belief in this book and her unfailing generosity have made it all possible.

My friend and colleague, Jack Clareman, has supported me in the writing of this book in more ways than I can name.

Like all therapists and teachers, I am gratefully aware that much of what I know I have learned from my clients and students.

Jonathan Cobb has for many years been my valued friend, writing teacher, and editor. He edited each chapter of this book; the reader will have cause to be thankful for his remarkable competence. It is to him this book is gratefully dedicated.

1

INTRODUCTION

*What is at stake in all these attacks? . . . The real object of attack—
for which Freud is only a stalking-horse—is the very idea that
humans have unconscious motivation. A battle may be fought over
Freud, but the war is over our culture's image of the human soul. Are
we to see humans as having depth—as complex psychological
organisms who generate layers of meaning which lie beneath the
surface of their own understanding? Or are we to take ourselves as
transparent to ourselves?*

—Jonathan Lear, *Open Minded*

It's not hard to find things to criticize in Freud's work. In his ringing defense of Freud, philosopher and psychoanalyst Jonathan Lear cheerfully acknowledges, "Freud botched some of his most important cases. Certainly a number of his hypotheses are false, his analytic technique can seem flat-footed and intrusive, and in his speculations he was a bit of a cowboy."[1] Many of the criticisms leveled against Freud are valid, and both his theories and his techniques are continually being refined and improved upon. Nevertheless, Freud radically changed the way many people look at themselves and their minds. His major insights, and those of his followers, can be extraordinarily instructive to us all and indispensable to clinicians.

Little Freudian or other psychodynamic theory is currently taught in our colleges. In most introductory psychology texts Freud is mentioned briefly and condescendingly as being of little more than historical interest. One of his books, almost always *Civilization and Its Discontents,* may be taught in an occasional "great books" program, and a smattering of anthropology and literature courses may include a bit of Freud. However, since his books were first published very few colleges have taught him as an important psychologist. Most academic authorities find his work unscientific and speculative and thus unfit for undergraduates. Those of us interested in unconscious motivation suspect that another reason is that those academic authorities find the theory of the unconscious unsettling.

Why is so little psychoanalytic theory now taught even to psychotherapy students? Between World War II and the 1960s most students of psychotherapy were taught a great deal of psychodynamic theory; they were not considered well trained without it. Now the pendulum has swung to the other side. What changed? Probably the best explanation is that Freud fell out of favor. Many feminists understandably objected to an unflattering picture of women, although it must be said that Freud didn't paint flattering pictures of anybody. The political consciousness of the 1960s saw Freud as a symbol of patriarchal oppression. Humanistic psychologists found him pessimistic. The 1960s was not the first period in which people turned away from Freud, however. His ideas have recurrently gone in and out of favor since his earliest presentations to the Vienna Medical Society in the 1800s.

There have been two forces struggling over the acceptance of Freud's ideas. The first is resistance to the upsetting nature of his theories, which has often driven them from favor. It is unsettling to have it suggested that our conscious minds are merely the tip of the iceberg and that the preponderance of our thoughts and feelings, and, above all, our motives, are hidden to us and sometimes neither benign nor innocent. It is as though we have believed we are characters in a mild drawing-room comedy and suddenly are asked to consider that we are actually cast in a poetic drama, wild and dark. The other force, which lies behind the periodic resurgence of Freudian ideas, has been the fascination of this very drama and the belief that learning about it could help reduce emotional suffering.

Freud's popularity has risen as well as fallen in various sub-cultures. After the period in the 1970s when many feminists found his ideas destructive, some important feminist sociologists and psychologists demonstrated that it was impossible to understand the foundations of sexism without understanding its unconscious dynamics. We will see later how Nancy Chodorow and Jessica Benjamin, two of the most sophisticated of these writers, integrate feminism and psychoanalysis. In the 1970s politically conscious therapists began to show how psychoanalysis could be made less authoritarian. They challenged the traditional view that the therapist was never wrong and the patient never right and developed a therapeutic ambience much friendlier and more humane then the traditional one. These therapists recognized that in the consulting room were two equal-status collaborators working for the patient's liberation. We entered a period when Freud was less often demonized.

In the history of psychoanalysis, however, every rise in popularity is followed by a decline. The 1990s saw a steady stream of books and articles claiming that modern neurology and psychopharmacology had made Freud irrelevant. The announcement of a Freud exhibit at the Library of Congress in 1998 created a remarkably emotional protest, one that would not have surprised Freud, who perhaps would have pointed out that so much emotion over a museum exhibit might be best explained by his theory.

One of the criticisms leveled at Freud by psychologists in the 1990s had to do with his biological orientation. Freud's roots in nineteenth-century biology led him to emphasize instinct and the inevitability of instinctual development. "Instinct" to Freud meant "need." An instinct was a need that was inherited by all humans and that demanded of the mind that it be satisfied. There were needs for food, sex, self-preservation, and so forth. Freud repeatedly classified and reclassified these instincts, searching for a way of understanding the basic human conflict as one between conflicting needs. At the end of his life he believed that all the instincts were ultimately subsumed under two major classifications, the life instinct and the death instinct. These were by definition opposed to each other, and it was the struggle between them that caused us such endless distress.

Another example of the effect of biological training on Freud's later ideas is his conceptualization of what he called the "latency period." Freud believed there was an inherited biological tendency for the sex drive to diminish markedly around the age of seven and return dramatically at puberty. This two-stage sex drive was one cause of the human tendency to neurosis. He thought that in the latency period the capacity for passion and the capacity for tenderness got out of synchrony, the tenderness trends continuing to develop while the passionate ones were stopped. As we will see in the pages ahead, this lack of synchrony ("Where I desire I cannot love; where I love I cannot desire") is one major cause of unhappiness. Few modern therapists deny that this problem exists, is common, and is distressing. However, few now accept Freud's biological explanation for it.

The conflict between life instincts and death instincts and the effects of the latency period are only two of many examples of Freud's biological orientation. In the argument about nature versus nurture, in many cases Freud was firmly on the side of nature, of instinct. The criticisms of this bias in Freud's thinking began early and have not subsided. It is argued that Freud neglected the impact of early experience, particularly children's early relationships with their caretakers. That argument is certainly justified. Freud's attention was taken up with his shattering insights into the early development of the unconscious, including instinctual drives, and he never did get to a real study of the effect of early relationships. The emphasis on those relationships, the study of "object relations," is a necessary and welcome addition to the study of psychodynamics.

Psychologists sometimes argue about "drive theory" versus "object relations" theory. This has never seemed to me a fruitful argument; they are both quite right. There is, for example, unmistakably a sex drive, and it is equally unmistakable that the expression of that drive is powerfully determined by our earliest relationships.

We have now begun to emerge from a long period during which many therapists thought they could do their work without making use of Freud's insights into the unconscious. There are schools of therapy, such as the behaviorists and the cognitive therapists, that still hold to that belief. However, outside of those specifically non-psychodynamic schools, more and more therapists now believe that whether or not Freud is fashionable, they cannot understand their clients without understanding the unconscious forces that shape their behavior.

One indication of the renewal of interest in Freud is the proliferation and popularity of psychoanalytic training institutes. San Francisco, for example, which for decades had only one such institute, now has four, and there are increasing numbers of applicants seeking training at them. Similar proliferation can be seen in New York and Los Angeles.

Perhaps, then, the reason for the repeated return of Freud from disfavor is that when all is said and done he is indispensable. He is indispensable to clinicians because, as I have said, it is difficult to understand a client without a working knowledge of unconscious processes and without the Freudian guides to the possible content of the client's unconscious. For example, without that knowledge and those guides, I would have been utterly baffled by my client, Sam.

> Sam is bewildered by his inability to commit to a woman. He tells me that such a commitment would feel like a betrayal. A betrayal of what or whom he cannot say. I remember that his beloved mother died when he was 12 and that his fondest memory is of her crying as, near the end of her life, she read him the ending of *Winnie the Pooh*. Christopher Robin knows he is getting too old to play with a teddy bear. He takes Pooh to a beautiful place in the forest and says, "Let's remember that at this place a boy and his bear will always be friends." Now I have a place from which to start; I have a connection that might help Sam make sense out this aspect of his life. I know that there is a connection in Sam's mind that is hidden from him. I think it may have to do with his grief over hav-

ing lost his mother and over a silent pact he believes they made before she died. I think it possible that he believes a commitment to a woman would constitute a betrayal of that silent pact. From Freud I have learned that connections like this are made without awareness, and, as we shall see in Chapter 4, I have learned a good deal about the likely relationship between a 12-year-old boy and his mother.

In *The Hero with a Thousand Faces*, Joseph Campbell reminds us of the beauty and power of being in touch with the underworld of our mind. In *Open Minded,* Jonathan Lear reminds us that it is a mistake to think of Freud as a mere healer of neurosis. He is a deep explorer of the human condition in a tradition that goes back to Sophocles and Shakespeare, and in that exploration finds that there are significant meanings for human well-being that are obscured from immediate awareness:

> It is a mistake to think of psychoanalysis and Prozac as different means to the same end. The point of psychoanalysis is to help us develop a clearer, yet more flexible and creative, sense of what our ends might be. "How shall we live?" is, for Socrates, the fundamental question of human existence—and the attempt to answer that question is, for him, what makes human life worthwhile. And it is Plato and Shakespeare, Proust, Nietzsche, and, most recently, Freud, who complicated the issue by insisting that there are deep currents of meaning, often cross-currents, running through the human soul which can at best be glimpsed through a glass darkly. This if anything, is the Western tradition: not a specific set of values, but a belief that the human soul is

too deep for there to be any easy answer to the question of how to live.[2]

The center of Freud's contribution is the depiction of the unconscious. The word "unconscious" has many meanings. It can mean *asleep;* it can mean *automatic*, such as stopping at a traffic light; it can mean *oblivious*, unaware of what's going on around one; it can mean *neurologically programmed,* as in hitting a baseball after much practice. When Freud used the word (and this is the way I use it in this book), he was talking about that part of our mental life, by far the largest part, of which we are unaware, those impulses and ideas, those wishes and fears, that operate out of sight and exert a powerful influence over our attitudes and behaviors.

Because so much of our mental life is hidden from us, we often remain in the dark about our underlying motives. When my client Alex decides to break up with his girlfriend, he tells himself it's because he's decided she isn't an interesting companion. That seems to him to be his motive. From what I know of Alex, Freud would suggest that he may never find a companion he decides is sufficiently "interesting" because there was a hidden motive for the breakup. The psychoanalytic theory of motivation is an attempt to clarify our reasons for doing what we do, for thinking what we think, for believing what we believe. Those behaviors, those thoughts, and those beliefs are to some extent—often to some *large* extent—the result of unconscious motivation. That is the subject of this book.

More often than not, clients are bewildered by their problems. They realize that their minds sometimes betray them and they don't understand why. That bewilderment is one important reason for seeking therapy. If they could make sense of their thoughts and feelings, their impulses and fears, their attitudes and their motives, they wouldn't need a therapist. The reason for that bewilderment is that much of their mental content is hidden to them, is unconscious. Therapists need a working knowledge of the unconscious to help their clients cast a light into those hidden realms. Although insight into those realms is seldom sufficient for clients' liberation—they also need some healing experience in the consulting room—it is certainly necessary.

The psychoanalytic theorist Robert Stolorow and his collaborators put it this way:[3] To make sense out of an overwhelming world, from early on we develop a group of *organizing principles*. The most basic of these become *invariant*, meaning that they are resistant to change, even in the face of contradictory evidence. Many of these are unconscious, either because they were formed very early in life or because they are linked to circumstances so emotionally threatening that they must be repressed. Someone who lost a loved parent early in life may well develop the unconscious principle that his or her love is dangerous. Someone who had a jealous parent may have developed the unconscious principle that it is forbidden to be beautiful. We all carry a substantial collection of invariant organizing principles of which we are unaware but that have a powerful influence on us. Stolorow teaches that a crucial aspect of therapy is making those invisible principles visible to give the client some choice about which are serviceable. Following are two examples of burdensome organizing principles.

> Arthur consults a therapist because of a recurrent need to sabotage himself whenever success seems imminent. As he tells his family history, one aspect stands out. As far back

as he can remember, he has been aware that there was something wrong with his younger brother. The boy had a very hard time in school, and it finally became clear to Arthur that his brother was retarded. It was also clear that his brother was the most loving person he knew and his best friend. Arthur went on to become a professional with graduate degrees, but in seeking to advance his career, he managed regularly to snatch defeat from the jaws of victory. In his work with the therapist it gradually became clear to him that his sadness over leaving his beloved brother farther and farther behind had developed into a kind of "survivor guilt" that contributed to the repeated sabotaging of any imminent success. His unconscious organizing principle was, "If success is not available to my brother, I am not entitled to it either."

The puzzled therapist begins to think that there is no way to please Deborah. She alternates complaints about the therapist's aloofness with complaints about her warmth. Eventually it becomes clear that Deborah's father was charming but emotionally unavailable, whereas her mother was loving, needy, and engulfing. Deborah enters therapy unconsciously believing that in every relationship these are the only two available choices. The therapist comes to understand that unconsciously Deborah alternately sees her as mother and as father. She is now in a position to help Deborah see how severely that principle has limited her expectations about the people in her life.

As it becomes clear that unconscious motivation is causing a client difficulty, the therapist has two tasks: try to make sense out of the unconscious dynamic that is causing the client such bewilderment, and, eventually, find a useful way to explain it to the client. To make sense out of the client's feelings and motives requires an understanding of unconscious dynamics. To be able to convey that understanding to the client in such a way that the client can make use of it is a delicate part of the craft of therapy. We will explore this further.

As I have mentioned, making the invisible motives visible is a necessary but not sufficient part of therapy. The subject of this book is unconscious motivation, understanding it and communicating it to the client. The other elements of therapy, crucial though they are, lie beyond the scope of this book. However, it is relevant to note what makes these other elements necessary. When Freud first discovered that his patients' symptoms represented unconscious motivations, he assumed that he could alleviate those symptoms by merely telling the patient what he had discovered. He was acutely disappointed. Such revelation rarely alleviated the symptom, or if it did, it did so only temporarily. Ever since, the history of psychotherapy has been an attempt to discover what must be added to insight to effect change. In the psychodynamic schools of therapy, most attempts to answer that question have focused on the quality of the relationship between therapist and client. We will have occasion to examine that quality when we consider the unconscious aspects of the clinical relationship in Chapter 11. For now, it is enough to note that although it almost certainly is not sufficient, the therapist's capacity to understand unconscious motivation and successfully communicate that understanding to the client is absolutely necessary.

Understanding therapy clients is not all that makes the study of unconscious motivation important. It is crucial for our self-understanding as well. Unconscious fear and guilt run our lives in unsuspected ways.

> Joanne is a healthy young married woman terrified of having a baby, certain she would die during delivery. She reports a dream that reminds her of an ancient legend that says that if you kill someone, be sure to avoid the scene of the murder because there the ghost of your victim has the power to kill you in revenge. She tells her therapist that her father was an obstetrician who died delivering a baby, and it soon becomes clear that for some as-yet-undetermined reason she feels responsible for her father's death and fears the consequences.

Strange connections are made in the unconscious. We react to one thing as though it were something else, and we react to a person as if he or she were someone else.

> Anthony's job requires close cooperation with a certain coworker. For years they have gotten along well and enjoyed working together. Lately there has been serious friction and Anthony accuses his coworker of being critical and aggressive; Anthony is sufficiently upset by his coworker's behavior to consider leaving a very good job. He and his therapist trace the problem to an incident in which he and his coworker had disagreed about something and had both expressed the disagreement with some heat. Gradually Anthony is helped to realize that he has refused to allow the bad feelings to subside. He acknowledges to his therapist that his coworker has tried to make peace several times and that he has resisted. After some

exploration, Anthony realizes that he is responding to the coworker in a pattern reminiscent of the way he did to his very angry and critical mother.

It is not unusual to discover that a situation about which we complain is one that we have in fact orchestrated, and that we therefore resist any attempt to change it. Marriages are notorious instances.

Karl and Katherine consult a couples therapist. Karl complains that Katherine is "frigid." Katherine shamefacedly agrees. They have previously consulted a sex therapist. The couples therapist inquires about what advice they were given. Katherine reveals that Karl had refused to follow the advice because he thought it useless. The therapist begins to wonder if Katherine was allowing herself to be labeled as sexually unavailable to protect Karl. And indeed, as they work together, the couple and the therapist discover that Karl has two deep-seated fears: He is afraid of being sexually inadequate and he is afraid that, should his partner be in touch with her passion, she will betray him with other men. None of this was conscious in either of them.

In Chapter 2 we'll see what Freud meant by the unconscious and what he taught us about it. Then we'll select, out of the large body of Freud's work (his writings fill 24 volumes!), those topics that best illuminate Freud's theory of the unconscious and that show how that theory can lead to greater self-understanding.

We'll explore Freud's theory of sexual development in Chapters 3 and 4, with particular attention to the Oedipus complex, which Freud considered the crown jewel of his theory. It is very hard for some people to find truly satisfactory mates to whom they can give and from whom they can receive both tenderness and passion. How does Freud help us understand that problem?

In Chapter 5 I describe the repetition compulsion, one of Freud's most powerful explanatory concepts.

In Chapters 6 through 8 we'll look at Freud's theories of anxiety and guilt and the theory of defense mechanisms: how we protect ourselves from anxiety. All of us seem to be frightened of ancient dangers, long past. We are likely to experience crippling guilt over mere wishes, wishes on which we have never acted. We limit our lives to a costly extent by concealing our deepest wishes from ourselves. How does Freud's theory of the unconscious illuminate those universal human phenomena?

Then we'll explore in Chapters 9 and 10 Freud's theory of dreams and of grief and mourning. One of the major contributions Freud made to clinical practice was the discovery of the consequences of unmourned loss. The paradox he unearthed is that attempting to avoid the pain of loss often leads to a greater and longer-lasting pain. Can we understand that paradox?

Chapter 11 covers a topic of central concern to every client and therapist: the unconscious aspects of the therapeutic relationship. The clinical relationship always turns out to be a good deal richer and more complicated than it appears—in both directions. This emerging complexity is of incomparable value to the client. How does that work?

2

THE UNCONSCIOUS

In one of his *Introductory Lectures,* Freud told the following story:

> I was once the guest of a young married couple and heard the young woman laughingly describe her latest experience. The day after her return from her honeymoon she had gone shopping with her unmarried younger sister while her husband went to his business. Suddenly she noticed a gentleman on the other side of the street, and nudging her sister had cried: "Look, there goes Herr L." She had forgotten that this gentleman had been her husband for some weeks. I shuddered as I heard the story, but I did not dare to draw the inference. The little incident only occurred to my mind some years later when the marriage had come to a most unhappy end.[1]

The inference Freud did not dare draw is clear: Although she may not have been consciously aware of it, the bride "knew" from the beginning that this was not a marriage she wanted to be in.

Freud did not discover the unconscious. The existence and importance of unconscious mental life had been considered by others before him and was being explored by at least one of his contemporaries. Poets and playwrights had long known of it, of course. What Freud did was add greatly to our knowledge of the contents and workings of unconscious processes and show how that knowledge could greatly increase the power both of therapists to help their clients and of all of us to understand the nature of our own psychic life and that of others.

The central statements of Freud's theory of the unconscious are not complicated: We don't know why we feel what we feel; we don't know why we fear what we fear; we don't know why we think what we think; and above all, we don't know why we do what we do. What we feel, fear, think, and do is much more complicated and much more interesting than it may at first appear.

We don't know why we feel what we feel.

> My adult client, Max, gets furious at his mother for incidents which, when he describes them, don't seem to me to remotely justify such intense reaction. It seems clear to me that something else must have triggered such anger.

We don't know why we fear what we fear.

> Marty reports that he takes every opportunity to avoid answering the telephone. When it becomes necessary to answer the phone he experiences typical symptoms of anxiety: His heart pounds, he sweats, his breathing becomes difficult. He has no idea why telephoning terrifies him.

We don't know why we think what we think.

Rebecca thinks she is unlovable. It makes no difference that people tell her they love her. She doesn't believe them and remains convinced she is unlovable.

We don't know why we do what we do.

George, who is a student, spends a weekend playing video games and flunks an important exam, one on which he could have done well with some effort. He reports that he got little pleasure from the games and actually is very interested in the course material he was supposed to study.

In one of his lectures Freud introduced the concept of the unconscious* by describing a patient who felt irresistibly compelled to hurry into a nearby room, stand by a certain table, and summon the parlor maid. She would then dismiss the maid but would soon feel compelled to repeat the sequence. The meaning of the ritual was a complete mystery to her and very distressing. Then one day she spontaneously understood it.

She was separated from her husband, with whom she had lived only briefly. On her wedding night her husband had been impotent. Through the course of the night he had repeatedly hurried from his room into hers, attempted intercourse, and failed. The next morning he had poured red ink on the bed so that the maid would believe his bride had been deflowered.

---

*There is an entire section of psychoanalytic history concerning the use of "unconscious" as an adjective and "the unconscious" as a part of the mind. Freud considered the term most useful as an adjective describing a quality of thought. I use it that way in this book, although occasionally I use it as a noun describing the entire collection of unconscious mental events, as in this sentence.

However, he hurriedly positioned the spot of ink in such a way that his stratagem was defeated.

Since the separation this woman had lived celibate and alone, her life crippled by obsessive rituals, thinking of her husband with exaggerated respect and admiration. She told Freud there was a stain on the cloth covering the table by which she stood when summoning the maid. She stood in such a way as to be sure the maid would see the stain.

The woman had unconsciously designed the ritual to save her husband from humiliation by symbolically showing the maid the hymenal spot on the sheet. When Freud first questioned her she had absolutely no idea of the meaning of the ritual. That is, it was unconscious.

With rare exception, psychologists before Freud thought of mental life and consciousness as synonymous. The idea of unconscious mental life seemed a contradiction in terms. Freud realized there was no way to explain the thoughts and actions of his patients without radically altering that view of the mind as a whole.

He saw that consciousness was only a small part of mental life, and conceived an image to describe the mind. He portrayed the unconscious as a large entrance hall filled with mental images, all trying to get into a small drawing room into which the entrance hall opens. In that drawing room resides consciousness, with whom the impulses are hoping for an audience. In the doorway between the entrance hall and the drawing room stands a watchman, whose job is examine each impulse seeking admission and decide if that impulse is acceptable. If it is not, the watchman turns it away, and it must remain in the entrance hall of unconsciousness. If an unacceptable impulse gets just past the threshold, the watchman will evict it and push it back into the entrance hall. The impulses that are turned back in this fashion are *repressed*. Once an impulse has gained admission to the drawing room, it still is not conscious until it has caught the eye of consciousness. Such impulses, those in the drawing room but not yet seen by consciousness, are *preconscious*; this drawing room is the system of the preconscious. This watchman who ejects, that is represses, unacceptable impulses is the same watchman who turns up as *resistance* when the analyst sets out to lift the repression for the liberation of the patient.[2]

The watchman might decide to refuse to admit an impulse or thought into the drawing room because if that impulse were to catch the eye of consciousness it would produce an unwelcome emotion: fear, guilt, or shame. We will examine those grounds for censorship in some detail in Chapter 6. For now it is enough to note that it is the job of the watchman-censor to apply those criteria as he screens applicants for admission to the drawing room.

Who are the inhabitants of the entrance hall, those thoughts, wishes, and impulses that make up unconscious mental life? The main attribute of the unconscious is, of course, that it is unconscious. For the purposes of this discussion, let's define an unconscious mental event as that to which one doesn't have verbal access, at least without unusual measures. If you ask me why I wasted the weekend joylessly, I really couldn't tell you. Nor could I tell you why I'm afraid of harmless mice. By applying special association techniques or perhaps taking sodium pentothal I might find out, but just sitting here trying to figure it out, I can't. Were these thoughts to become conscious they would cause a painful feeling. Therefore they are being forcibly kept in the entrance hall by the watchman.

The impulses and thoughts in the drawing room upon which the eye of consciousness has not alighted constitute the preconscious. Freud defined this as a mental event, not presently conscious, but capable of being called to consciousness at will. It is not likely that at this moment you are thinking of your mother's maiden name, but should I ask you what it is, you could probably call it up and report it. Until you called it up it was preconscious. Some unconscious things are more deeply buried than others. The watchman has instructions to be more stringent about rejecting some impulses than others. For example, I seem to have trouble remembering the name of a certain orchestra conductor. Right now, I couldn't tell you what it is. But if I work at it, perhaps by going through the alphabet until I reach the first letter of his name, I can almost always recover it. Right now that information is unconscious, but not very. On the other hand, I'm certain that there are memories and feelings, probably very old ones, buried so deeply and so well guarded that it is unlikely I will ever access them. Many of our motives are somewhere in between. They are possible to access, but not easy.

Freud recognized that many ideas are simply forgotten and not repressed at all. Forgotten ideas drift away and are gone. Ideas repressed into the unconscious remain a part of the person's mental life. Therapists who insist that *everything* is motivated are notorious for getting into fruitless arguments with their clients. It is not always easy or productive to attempt to distinguish between that which is repressed and that which is simply forgotten.

Freud drew a sharp line between preconscious and unconscious. If something could be readily accessed it was simply preconscious; if not it was unconscious. In practice, however, it often seems difficult to make that clear distinction between those categories. I think the most workable model is that of a continuum of ideas from conscious to deeply buried. "Preconscious" would refer to those ideas just below consciousness on the continuum.

Another important feature of unconscious mental events is that, whereas conscious events obey the laws of "secondary process," much, although not all, of the unconscious is governed by the laws of what Freud called "primary process." Secondary process describes the familiar world of logic. Events occur in an orderly sequence. What's past is past and what's future has not yet come. This is the world of cause and effect. If I study I get good grades; if I am irritable with a friend he is likely to be irritated. In this world fantasy and action are different things with different consequences. If I daydream instead of cleaning the room, I am aware it will not actually get clean. If I wish something bad to happen to someone, I don't think it's my fault if, by coincidence, something does.

Unlike secondary process, primary process operates without regard for *reality*. This implies a strange kind of logic, not the logic we know in the realm of secondary process. In this realm there is no concept of mutual contradiction or mutual exclusion. I might want to kill my father and have him take me to the movies tomorrow. I expect you to love me after I've insulted you. The laws of reality and logic being so loose, strange associations can exist: An idea can stand for a similar one; one idea can be displaced onto a totally different one; one idea can stand for a whole group of ideas.

My fear of my father can become fear of a horse biting me. This is a typical association chain in the realm of primary process: I love and fear my father. I am conscious of the love but the fear is unconscious. I am afraid he will hurt me physically to punish me for bad thoughts. A horse is a large, intimidating figure like my father. I have seen the horse's dangerous teeth. I'm not consciously afraid of my father but rather of the horse. That has advantages: Horses are easier to avoid than my father.

My anger at a parent can become a radical political position. My parents use their authority to restrict me. The government is also an authority. I will direct my rebelliousness at the government. My longing for my comforting mother can become a fondness for a class of foods. (It is no accident that foods such as mashed potatoes and warm custard are called "comfort foods.")

Primary process is timeless. It recognizes no past and no future. If something was dangerous 20 years ago, it is still dangerous. If I am suffering now, I will always suffer. If, long ago, I was afraid my parents would punish me for bad thoughts or bad acts, the fear of that punishment remains in full force even after my parents are long dead. One of the goals of psychodynamic therapy is to take the important issues out of the realm of primary process and into the realm of secondary process. If I begin therapy burdened by this fear, my therapist and I will be pleased if I learn (deeply) that there is no longer anything to fear, that there is no authority wanting to punish me.

In the realm of primary process there is no distinction between fantasy and reality, between wish and action. If I want my father dead I might be as guilty as if I had killed him. Should he actually die from some totally unrelated cause, I am convinced I killed him, and the guilt is severe. Similarly, should I long for a pleasure I believe is bad, I might be as guilty as if I had actually experienced it. Freud thought that the guilt over an unconscious wish could be stronger and more destructive than the guilt over an actual act. Ironically, for most of us, although the guilt may be as great, the fantasy *pleasure* is not as satisfying as it would have been in reality.

Perhaps most important, primary process operates on the "pleasure principle." The pleasure principle requires *pleasure! now!* It is the opposite of the "reality principle" on which secondary process operates. Freud thought that when infants experience a need, they imagine the food or the event or the person that will meet that need. Soon they learn the inadequacy of this way of getting needs met and discover that they must attend to, and learn the rules of, the external world, of *reality.* Imagining milk does not reduce the hunger. Imagining mother's presence does not provide enough comfort. Babies learn the necessity of manipulating the real world to satisfy their wants. This is the beginning of the reality principle.

As the child grows, this principle becomes increasingly sophisticated. Under its sway children learn the advantages (sometimes the *necessity*) of *delaying gratification.* Most second graders, if asked whether they want a small candy bar now or a large one tomorrow, choose the small one now. They are operating under the influence of the pleasure principle: pleasure *now* and no delay! Many third graders, on the other hand, will choose to wait for the large candy bar. Between the ages of seven and eight children learn the advantage of delaying gratification.

As the reality principle develops, children learn to estimate consequences. I don't feel like doing homework, but I choose not to incur the teacher's displeasure and possible punishment. As we will see in the pages ahead, one of the most powerful inhibitors of pleasure-seeking behavior is fear of being punished by our conscience: fear of guilt. There is often nothing to stop me from hurting a powerless person except my awareness of the severe pain my conscience would inflict upon me. Freud thought that this is what prevents civilized life from becoming even more destructive and dangerous than it presently is.

As we grow, we apply the reality principle to more and more sophisticated issues. A scientist rejects a research project that she could finish relatively quickly and easily, choosing instead a more challenging one. Athletes, dancers, and singers put themselves through years of grueling practice to meet a standard of excellence.

Freud made an interesting observation about the sexual impulses in relation to the pleasure and reality principles. Because the sex drive, unlike some others, is capable of solitary satisfaction, satisfaction that doesn't require reality testing, delay of gratification, or concern for consequences, in some people it comes less under the sway of the reality principle than do other drives and thus is apt to cause the person a great deal of pain and trouble. That trouble can take many forms. In some it can lead to never giving up masturbation as the main method of satisfaction; in others it can lead to disastrous sexual adventures, when a moment's thought would have made the consequences apparent. Perhaps that is why it has proven so hard to stem the spread of sexually transmitted diseases. Perhaps this concept could be broadened to include other drives, including the hunger drive, to throw some light on the prevalence and tenacity of eating disorders.

The pleasure principle is *pleasure! now!* and the reality principle is *safer pleasure later, even if it's less pleasure.* Were it not for the development of the reality principle we would continuously be in serious trouble. We would have no capacity to delay gratification, estimate consequences, or assess reality.

There is always a tug of war between the pleasure principle and the reality principle. It is remarkable that Robert Louis Stevenson wrote *Dr. Jekyll and Mr. Hyde* without knowing Freud's work. It is a gripping story of the pleasure principle and the reality principle. Dr. Jekyll, feeling the constraints of civilized life, devises a potion that will allow him to act out the impulses of the pleasure principle, impulses that exist in the unconscious of us all. Dr. Jekyll is as sweet and gentle a man as can be found in London society. When his unconscious impulses are allowed to see the light of day, we learn that they are concerned only with instant gratification. They recognize no delay and, disastrously, they recognize no concern for the well-being of others. When Dr. Jekyll takes the potion he becomes Mr. Hyde, a cruel, totally selfish monster, his sexual and aggressive impulses unrestrained.

Presented in this way, the world of primary process sounds horrible and, as in Mr. Hyde, if unrestrained it can be disastrous. However, there is another, equally important, side to the picture. The realm of primary process contains the raw material for our poetry, our creativity, and our playfulness. A world of pure secondary process would be a sterile world indeed. Freud taught that the artist is one who can explore the realm of primary process and then make an artistic unity out of what is found there. He might have added that the same applies to the passionate lover and the imaginative companion.

In Freud's original conception, the mind was composed of three systems: the *unconscious*, the *preconscious,* and the *perceptual-conscious*. We have already met that model in the picture of the drawing room, the entrance hall, and the watchman. The unconscious system (the entrance hall) was the realm of primary process and the pleasure principle, and the conscious system (the drawing room) was the seat of secondary process and the reality principle. It eventually became clear to Freud that although this was a good way to think of repression and the relationship of consciousness to the unconscious, a complete theory of the mind required a different model. He had always seen the human mind as being in persistent, unremitting conflict, and it seemed to him that his clinical data could be handled best by a picture of the mind divided not into the original three systems but into three agencies, often struggling with each other. In his final model one of those agencies operated under the laws of primary process and the pleasure principle, and another under the laws of secondary process and the reality principle. In his final picture the three agencies in the mind are the *id*, the *ego*, and the *superego.*

The id is the repository of the instinctual drives, sexual and aggressive. It is totally unconscious and totally unsocialized. It always operates on the pleasure principle, demanding satisfaction of the drives completely and without delay. It does not care for consequences, reason, or good sense, nor does it care about the well-being of others. The id is what Dr. Jekyll's potion released, and the resulting Mr. Hyde is a chilling picture of the id run wild. As well as operating on the pleasure principle, the id follows the laws of primary process, with no sense of time or mutual exclusion.

The superego is our conscience. It represents our having taken into our own mind the standards and prohibitions of our parents and of society. Originally we feared losing the love and protection of our parents if we gave way to the impulses of the id. Once we have taken those standards and prohibitions into ourselves, we have to be aware of a new set of consequences: the attack on us by the superego, which is to say, *guilt.* Part of the superego is conscious; we know a lot about what our conscience permits and forbids. However, a large part of it is unconscious, giving rise to one of our most difficult and destructive problems: unconscious guilt.

The ego is the executive function. It is given the thankless task of mediating among the id, the superego, and the outside world. It operates according to the laws of secondary process and the reality principle. In contradistinction to the id, it is concerned with consequences and does its best to delay gratification to avoid trouble or to gain a greater gratification later. As Freud put it, "The ego stands for reason and good sense while the id stands for untamed passions."[3]

Because the ego manages relations with the outside world, to get its passions gratified the id must enlist the services of the ego. The ego is thus under continual pressure from the id. It must serve two additional masters as well. It must decide whether an action dictated by the id will meet with danger or punishment in the external world and whether it will escape punishment from the superego, that is, the pangs of guilt. It also functions as the watchman in the model of the drawing room and entrance hall, taking on the task of repression and other modes of defense against anxiety. The part of the ego responsible for these defense mechanisms resides in the unconscious.

To Freud, mental health depends in large part on the strength and flexibility of the ego. If it mediates wisely, giving the maximum possible satisfaction to its two internal masters and staying out of trouble with its external one; if it represses no more than is necessary; if it has a great deal of its energy available for joyful and creative living, then the person has escaped the neurosis that so much of civilized life is heir to. I mentioned previously the importance of being able to journey into the underworld of primary process and then creatively organize the resulting discoveries. The Freudians call this process "regression in the service of the ego."

Mr. Hyde presents us with evidence for the necessity of repression. Because the id is a cauldron of impulses, many of them unsocialized, we would be in serious trouble without some optimal amount of repression. We would either be in jail or terribly frustrated because of the endless need to suppress our wishes. Too little repression is not a good condition. Well, how about too much? It seems likely that this is a problem for every reader of this book, certainly for its author. Freud thought it was the condition of most members of a civilized society. Too much repression involves a number of serious costs:

1. If repressed impulses and wishes, repressed organizing principles, all live their lives out of reach of my conscious control, out of sight of the ego, I cannot choose how to deal with them. I cannot choose whether or not to act on them. I cannot remind myself that these are relevant to, say, a five-year-old, not an adult. I cannot apply the reality principle and opt for short-term pain. Thus my life is severely circumscribed by organizing principles that no longer serve me, ones I cannot see, let alone change.

2. Repressed ideas keep their full emotional charge forever. What seemed very dangerous many years ago will seem equally dangerous as long as it is repressed.

3. Repressed wishes and impulses are under pressure, seeking expression. It is necessary to exert psychic energy to maintain the repression. The ego's job includes organizing, focusing, and implementing one's life, including love, work, play, and learning. That's quite a

job; the more energy my ego has at its disposal for those jobs, and the less energy is siphoned off in the service of repression, the better off I am. Otherwise I am like an army with so many of my troops on guard duty that there is no one available to fight.

4. Repressed ideas attract similar ideas into repression, and thus the area of the repressed grows. Psychologists who study the laws of learning think of this as *stimulus generalization.* If I teach you to press a button when you see a red light, you are very apt to press the button if I show you a very pink light. I learned as a child that it was dangerous to be assertive to my parents, so I repressed assertive impulses. As I grew up and confronted situations in which it would be adaptive to be assertive, I repressed the impulse because it felt dangerously like the original one. Thus my fear of being assertive progressively spread to more and more situations and became more and more inhibiting.

When Freud first discovered the existence and importance of unconscious mental life, he found himself addressing colleagues who had been taught that all mental life was conscious. He was challenged to provide evidence and typically offered three kinds: dreams, neurotic symptoms, and what he termed *parapraxes* (slips of the tongue and other similar mistakes).

Dreams

Freud called dreams the royal road to the unconscious. He meant that once the interpreter understood the way dreams work, they would reveal the most important unconscious wishes. This he saw not only as evidence for the existence of unconscious mental life but as a major therapeutic tool. Following is an example from *Introductory Lectures*:

> A lady who, though she was still young, had been married for many years had the following dream: She was at the theatre with her husband. One side of the orchestra was completely empty. Her husband told her that Elise L. and her fiancé had wanted to go too, but had only been able to get bad seats—three for 62 cents—and of course they could not take those. She thought it would not really have done any harm if they had.[4]

It is important to remember that Freud thought a dream could be analyzed only with the associations of the dreamer; they would reveal the hidden meaning. Following are a few of the dreamer's associations and the interpretation:

- Elise was about the dreamer's age and had just become engaged, although the dreamer herself had been married for 10 years.
- The dreamer had been in a hurry to reserve seats for a play last week and when she got there found half the orchestra empty; *there had been no need to be in such a hurry.*
- The 62 cents: Her sister-in-law had been given a present of $62.00 and *had been in a great hurry—the silly goose*—to rush off to the jewelers' and buy a piece of jewelry.
- *Three* seats: *The newly engaged Elise was only three months her junior, although the dreamer herself had been a married woman for 10 years.*

- *The interpretation*: It was absurd of me to be in such a hurry to get married. I can see from Elise's example that *I* could have got a husband later, too. And I could have gotten one a hundred times better (the relation between 62 cents and $62.00).[5]

Neurotic Symptoms

It is difficult to account for self-destructive behavior without positing an unconscious mental life. People adopt behaviors, attitudes, and inhibitions that cripple their lives; they sincerely report that they have no idea why they do such things to themselves. Freud described the following case:

A 19-year-old woman gradually acquires a collection of bedtime rituals that take hours to complete and that drive her and her parents to despair. She would give anything to be able to relinquish them, yet she feels desperately compelled to perform them perfectly. The pillows must be arranged precisely so that they don't touch the headboard, for example. After a great deal of psychoanalytic work Freud and his patient discover that the headboard represents man and the pillow woman. They then discover that the ritual represents the injunction that mother and father must not touch each other. Indeed, it turns out that before she developed these rituals, as a young child she had insisted that the door between her room and her parents' room must be left open, ostensibly to soothe her anxieties. Actually, she wanted to be able to monitor and thus prevent any sexual activity. The analysis eventually revealed that she had from early childhood been in the grip of an erotic attachment to her father and an angry jealousy of her mother.[6]

Parapraxes

By parapraxes Freud meant slips: of the tongue, of the pen, and various kinds of forgettings and bungled actions. He was fascinated by these phenomena and found them a wonderful window into the workings of the unconscious. Early in his career he collected examples and published them in *The Psychopathology of Everyday Life.*[7] He thought parapraxes a clear and convincing way of introducing newcomers to the idea of the unconscious and opened his *Introductory Lectures* with a long description of the phenomenon.

Freud's theory of parapraxes will not surprise a reader who has come this far. A person *intends* something: to say something, to remember something, to do something. But there is a competing intention, one that the watchman attempts to censor. Impulses denied are impulses under pressure, and here the rejected impulse finds a way of getting expressed by causing the slip. Following is one of Freud's examples from *The Psychopathology of Everyday Life:*

Freud and a friend are commiserating about anti-Semitism, which the friend finds particularly frustrating. He ends a passionate speech with a well-known line of Virgil's in which the unhappy Dido, having been abandoned by Aeneas, commits to posterity her vengeance. Or rather, he attempts to end his speech that way; he cannot remember the whole line. The line he attempts to quote is, *"Exoriare aliquis nostris ex ossibus ultor,"* which means, "Let someone arise from my bones as an avenger." However, he omits the word, "aliquis" (someone) and can't recover it, although the quote is one he knows well and has kept in memory since his school days. Freud supplies the missing word and induces him to give his associations to the memory lapse. The friend first finds that he wants to divide the word "aliquis" into two parts: "a" and "liquis." His chain of associations then produces: *"Relics, liquefying, fluidity, fluid, St. Januarius and the miracle of his blood."* Freud inquires and his friend responds, "They keep the blood of St. Januarius in a phial inside a church in Naples, and on a particular holy day it miraculously liquefies. The people attach great importance to this miracle and get very excited if it's delayed, as happened once at a time when the French were occupying the town. So the general in command . . . took the reverend gentleman aside and gave him to understand, with an unmistakable gesture toward the soldiers posted outside, that he *hoped* the miracle would take place very soon. And in fact it did take place." He pauses in embarrassment and Freud needs to urge him to continue. "Well, then, I've suddenly thought of a lady from whom I might easily hear a piece of news that would be very awkward for both of us."

Freud: "That her periods have stopped?"

"How could you guess that?"

"Think of . . . the blood that starts to flow on a particular day, the disturbance when the event fails to take place, the open threat that the miracle must be vouchsafed, or else. . . . In fact you've made use of the blood miracle of St.

Januarius to manufacture a brilliant allusion to a woman's periods."[8]

I find this a particularly useful example because of its demonstration of the ingenuity of the unconscious. Freud's friend had intended to ask for descendants to avenge him. That was his conscious intention, but the wish for descendants brought up the realization that he was in no position just now to indulge in that wish. A descendant was the last thing he wanted under these circumstances. The fear of his girlfriend's pregnancy remained unconscious, and from the unconscious that fear expressed itself by blocking out the word "aliquis," just the "someone" he didn't want. Once allowed to play with the associations, the unconscious constructed a creative path that enabled Freud to interpret the slip.

We have seen, in this chapter, something of the nature of the unconscious and how we are motivated by it. In the next two chapters we'll turn to the realm in which those unconscious motivations are most powerful and bewildering, the realm of our sexuality.

James Strachey, Freud's English translator, introduces his translation of Freud's major work on sexuality with these words: "Freud's *Three Essays on Sexuality*[9] stands, there can be no doubt, beside his *Interpretation of Dreams* as his most momentous and original contributions to human knowledge." That seems to me a fair assessment. Freud's studies of infantile sexuality, of psychosexual development, of the role of sex in causing neurosis, and, perhaps above all, of the Oedipus complex, have changed our view of humankind to an unimaginable degree.

3

PSYCHOSEXUAL DEVELOPMENT

It is astonishing that the human race could have for so long clung to the belief that children were asexual beings.
—Sigmund Freud, *Introductory Lectures*

Before the publication of Freud's *Three Essays on the Theory of Sexuality* it was accepted as a matter of course in European society that sex began at puberty. It was unthinkable that the innocence and purity of children could be accompanied by sexual wishes, fantasies, and pleasures. It was even more unthinkable that those fantasies might sometimes be about parents. It isn't surprising that the reverberations of Freud's book shook the Western world. His argument had two major implications: The sexual wishes, fantasies, and pleasures of children begin almost at birth and continue, except perhaps for a brief period, throughout the person's life; and emotional problems of children and adults most often have their roots in this early sex life.

Freud used the phrase "polymorphously perverse" to describe the earliest pleasures of children, which are obtained by them from organs other than genital. By that he meant that every bodily pleasure that will later become the primary choice of adults called perverts is included in the repertory of young children. Freud asserted that he was altogether justified in calling these bodily pleasures sexual because they so clearly contain the seeds of adult sexuality, and also because relatively early in life they center around genital pleasure and wishes for contact with another person.

These views of Freud's, like his views of the unconscious, grew out of endless hours of listening to patients. Freud's patients "free-associated," meaning that they did their best to say every thought that came into their minds, even if it seemed irrelevant or embarrassing to them at the time. Freud and his colleagues sat, often silent, and listened hour after hour, day after day, year after year. In the whole history of human relations nobody, no parent or lover, no priest or doctor, may ever have listened like that over such a sustained period. It is not surprising that the therapists heard things no one had heard or understood before.

Based on these associations and the memories his patients recalled, Freud hypothesized that the sexuality of children passes through a succession of developmental stages in the first 13 or so years of life, each of which is characterized by preoccupation with a different part of the body. This journey, the parents' responses to these stages, and how the child deals with those responses, Freud argued, have lifelong effects.

Because those responsible for the child's upbringing almost always make it clear to the child that sexual wishes and fantasies are forbidden, the watchman of the mind is ordered to exclude them from consciousness. Thus they become an important and particularly influential part of the unconscious and a major source of unconscious motivation.

> A client responds to a personal rejection by going to the local ice cream parlor and eating a large sundae topped with whipped cream.

> Another client spends a great deal of her time and energy futilely trying to cope with an extraordinarily chaotic and messy apartment.

> A male client longing for a relationship lives a solitary life occupied with his sports car and his collection of cameras. (The comedian Mort Sahl once said, "Anyone who loves watches and fast cars doesn't need people.")

Any of us not trained to think in terms of psychosexual development could be puzzled by all of these behaviors. Freud's theory is illuminating.

It has now been almost 100 years since Freud published his theory of psychosexual stages. As we enter the twenty-first century, there is, among psychodynamic theorists, a wide range of attitudes toward the theory of psychosexual stages. Certainly every clinician now believes that early relationships with the people in our environment have a great impact on our subsequent development. There is also no question that the more recent theories of early object relations and early interactional patterns are essential additions to Freud's original drive theory. It seems likely that Freud would have welcomed these additions; his own work was unmistakably heading in this direction.

The controversies today center around the question of emphasis. Students in the more orthodox psychoanalytic institutes are still taught the primacy of the psychosexual stages. Those stages are discussed, but less emphasized, in "object relations" institutes. In the growing number of institutes that emphasize the central therapeutic importance of the relationship between therapist and client, that is, the "relational" institutes, an increasingly creative effort is being made to synthesize the various points of view. Regardless of the remaining differences, there is growing agreement about some basic ideas. Most therapists now see the recognition of infantile sexuality as a major contribution, and most understand psychological difficulties as residues of problems at a particular maturational phase. Freud's clinical observations and his resulting theory of psychosexual stages were the remarkably insightful origins of this attitude, and therefore his theory is still important to understand.

In the Freudian typology, at each of the stages children pass through, one part of the body and the activities associated with it take on particular importance, one aspect of which is the pleasure provided by that body part. The stages are

- the oral period (from birth to about 18 months);
- the anal period (from 18 months to about three years);
- the phallic period and Oedipus Complex I (from three years to about seven years);
- the latency period (from seven years to puberty);
- Oedipus Complex II (at puberty); and
- the genital period (from puberty on).

These stages don't end and begin sharply in a person's life; rather, each tends to fade into and overlap with the next. The timetable is also approximate and variable. Not only do the stages overlap, they also persist, unconscious and hidden, as ongoing background to subsequent stages.

Freud was strongly influenced by contemporary developments in biology and tended to think like a biologist. He therefore saw psychosexual development as an instinctual unfolding within the individual. Much of the work done by Freud's followers has put his work in more of an interpersonal context. There is no doubt that there are instincts, although there is endless disagreement over how best to classify them. Similarly, there is no doubt that at some level there is a built-in maturation timetable. But at each moment along the way the developing child meets new interpersonal challenges, tasks, and responses. Each instinct serves as the raw material that is shaped by these challenges, tasks, and parental responses. This process has a powerful effect on the growing child. This post-Freudian interpersonal emphasis—the emphasis on the child's early "object relations"—has greatly enriched Freud's theories in general; the theory of psychosexual development is no exception.

Depending on how the parents respond, each stage can be gratifying for the child and interesting to the parents, or it can be difficult, perhaps even very difficult. Whether it's gratifying or difficult will have a lasting effect on the child, as will the specific modes of parental response.

Fixation and Regression

Freud's model of the mind included the idea that there exists a quantity of psychic energy that can be directed and redirected, a particularly important concept to keep in mind when considering the various psychosexual stages. (Freud's original English translator, James Strachey, invented the word "cathexis" as a name for this energy.) When a large amount of this energy is directed to an idea or a wish or a memory, that idea or wish takes on two characteristics: It becomes important and it becomes charged with emotion. As children enter each psychosexual stage in turn, they invest a large quantity of energy in the wishes and pleasures of that stage. In normal development, as they move on they withdraw a certain amount of that energy and direct it to the next stage. Fixation refers to an unusual amount of energy being left behind. In the unconscious, a stage at which one is fixated retains some large part of the importance and emotion it originally had. Thus it is the comfortable psychic place to which to *regress* if the going gets rough.

Regression describes returning to a point of fixation when a person is frustrated or frightened. Just as fixation can be to a psychosexual stage or to a relationship, so regression can take us back to either of those. (We will examine regression more closely after discussing the psychosexual stages.)

Fixation was Freud's way of describing the lasting effect on the child when the parental response is less than optimal. If the child's experiences in a given stage are very traumatic (or excessively overindulgent), the lessons learned or inferred during that period become deeply implanted. Fixation can also refer to an early relationship or a stage of an early relationship. It is common for someone to be unconsciously fixated on his or her relationship with a parent. If I am fixated in that way, a good deal of my psychic energy is engaged in longing for that person or trying to excise the pain of that relationship.

Early relationships are very powerful and, because they are written on a relatively clean slate, they tend to be enduring. If my childhood fixation is very strong, it is difficult for me to bring much of myself to an adult relationship, and it is difficult to see the people in my adult life as other than stand-ins for early characters.

The legendary Don Juan goes from woman to woman, his need for variety apparently insatiable. Psychoanalytic observers of this story suggest that it is not actually variety he is seeking. Don Juan represents mother fixation: It is she he is hopelessly and futilely seeking.

My client Barbara had an emotionally distant father. She tried without success throughout her childhood to get his attention and make some emotional connection with him. The deprivation and frustration of that crucial relationship were powerfully fixating. Now she chooses one emotionally distant boyfriend after another in an unconscious attempt to heal that first relationship by finally getting a cold man to love her.

Infantile Sexuality

Very young children are led to the discovery of sensual pleasure by engaging in necessary bodily functions. The first of these is the taking of nourishment. The mouth, lips, and tongue are very sensitive; stimulating them is, to the infant, very pleasurable. The next to appear are the functions of elimination, particularly defecation. The skin around the anus is very sensitive and capable of giving pleasure. Finally, the child discovers the genitals and the intense pleasure that can be had by stimulating them. Freud described all of these pleasures as auto-erotic because only the self is necessary for their enjoyment.

Oral Period

Because the child's first concerns have to do with the intake of nourishment, it is no surprise that the oral period comes first. The child quickly learns that sucking is pleasurable even when there is no milk. This leads to thumb sucking or sucking some other part of the body.

The mouth also seems to be the first source of pleasure. Babies do much of their early exploring of the world with their mouths. The earliest frustrations are the oral ones: hunger, thirst, and an unsatisfied need to suck. The mouth also serves as an early organ for aggression: biting, yelling, and crying. These pleasures first teach a child that bliss can be had when one is totally alone. Nobody else need be present. Mother is needed for milk, but sucking one's thumb or other body part or even a blanket is pleasurable as well. These pleasures are largely repressed as the child grows, but they remain powerful in the unconscious. It's not hard to see why, when the interpersonal going gets rough in later life, there can be strong temptation to go back to a time when I didn't need anyone.

Parental Response

Many years ago, the prevailing pediatric advice was to feed the child on a schedule. If the child began to cry for the breast or bottle three hours before her scheduled feeding, she cried for three hours. I myself was raised this way; I don't recommend it. Then the prevailing wisdom changed to "demand" feeding. When the baby was hungry, he got fed. It's not hard to imagine what lessons are being taught about the world under these two regimes. Feeding on schedule is an early and therefore powerful statement to the child that her interests and needs are not as important as the convenience of others. Demand feeding, on the other hand, teaches that he has the right to ask for what he needs and be confident that those needs will often be met. Scheduled feeding is apt to make her pessimistic about what rights she has in the world; demand feeding is more likely to make him an optimist.

Parents can have a wide variety of responses to non-nutrient sucking, such as thumb sucking. They might leave it alone and let the child find her own way to grow out of it, or they can take severe measures to stop it. Such measures include tying the child's hands, putting a little cage on the thumb, telling the child he's doing a bad thing, and punishing him. These are the child's earliest lessons about the parents' attitude toward her having pleasure. She may well generalize this attitude to all pleasures, particularly bodily pleasures.

The other major issue of parental response to the oral period is weaning. Is it done early or late? Is it done abruptly or gradually? Is it done at the child's initiative or the parents'? The answers to those questions contain lessons for the child about the world into which he has been born, and, because they come so early, they are apt to be extraordinarily influential.

Oral Fixation

Orally fixated people may develop a serious eating disorder, anorexia, bulimia, or overeating; they may tend to eat when stressed or lonely; they may be passive and dependent. They may prefer oral sex to other kinds. They may be orally aggressive, which for adults probably means verbally "biting" but for children can mean literally biting. The passivity and dependency of people with severe oral fixations can cause them (and the people close to them) real distress. Mild oral fixation often seems so common as to be universal. It's instructive to watch a room full of college students taking an exam. It would be rare to see someone actually sucking his thumb, but recognizable substitutes are common.

Anal Period

In the second year, children show considerable interest in feces and defecation. There is pleasure in defecation and pleasure in withholding it. In addition to these pleasures, children often learn from their parents the inadvertently taught lesson that feces is a gift that can be given or withheld. Defecation becomes a topic of major interpersonal concern: The parents have plans for this function that may not readily fit with the child's interests.

The associations of Freud's patients led him to the realization that this period included the appearance of sadism. In fact he often called it the "sadistic-anal period." It is likely to be the time when children are angered by the restrictions of socialization. Children at this age are developing teeth and thus the capacity to hurt by biting. They are also growing stronger and feeling their physical power. During this stage the sexual and aggressive instincts are becoming linked. This linkage may be entirely repressed later and remain in the unconscious, or, as in many people, it will remain at least partly conscious, leading to sadistic and masochistic sexual fantasies and behaviors.

Parental Response

The parental attitude toward feces and defecation is a powerful teacher. The child can learn that the body, its functions, and its products are natural and unobjectionable, or he can learn that they are disgusting and shameful. Toilet training is also a powerful teacher, a major instance of being taught to live in society. Toilet training can be early and severe or essentially nonexistent, with the child allowed to wear diapers without comment until he decides he wants out of them. Or it can be anything in between. Early and severe toilet training teaches that things are to be done the parents' way, not the child's. Relaxed or nonexistent toilet training bespeaks parental confidence in the child's ability to figure things out.

For many children this is the point at which they learn that there is a serious conflict between their pleasure-seeking nature and the demands of their parents. The importance for later development of the internalization of this conflict cannot be overemphasized. Freud cites with approval a paper by his colleague, Lou Andreas Salome:

> It is the first prohibition which the child receives—the prohibition against getting pleasure from anal activity and its products. This has a decisive effect on his whole development. This must be the first occasion when the child has a glimpse of an environment hostile to his instinctual impulses, an occasion on which he learns to separate his own entity from this alien one, and on which he carried out his first repression of his possibilities for pleasure. From that time on what is "anal" remains the symbol of everything that is to be repudiated and excluded from life.[1]

Anal Fixation

Anal fixation can take different forms. The most common appears to be compulsiveness. The child has learned that failing to "put things in their proper place" or failing to keep order is grounds for chastisement. Therefore she attempts to keep her anxiety level low by maintaining an orderly control of her environment. The trait of compulsiveness can vary in intensity. There is a normal amount necessary to keep one's life in order. (No one gets very far in higher education without enough compulsiveness to keep notes organized and make it to class on time.) At the other end of the continuum is a full-blown obsessive-compulsive disorder, in which obsessions and compulsions seriously interfere with one's life. One of Freud's most famous patients could not rid himself of the graphically agonizing mental picture of something horrible happening to his loved ones. He was also recurrently paralyzed by trivial compulsions, things that he "must do." ("I must take that stone out of the road. . . . Oh, I've made a mistake; I must go back and replace that stone.")

Anally fixated people who are compulsively clean often (perhaps always) unconsciously crave the dirt, messiness, and disorder they so scrupulously avoid. I used to conduct personal-growth groups, often attended by conventional, middle-class, middle-aged people, most of them properly neat and orderly. One of our regular activities was a finger-painting session. It was instructive, and I must say enjoyable, to watch (or participate in). The participants would begin delicately and carefully spreading the paint on the paper with their fingertips, and before long, with joyful abandon, they would be smearing paint on themselves and each other. Afterward they would typically report that even as children they had not permitted themselves that kind of uninhibited fun.

Freud observed that people with anal fixations were apt to be "orderly, parsimonious, and stubborn." "Orderly" seems easy to understand. If we recall that where and when the child defecates is the first big struggle, we can certainly understand "stubborn." As he listened to his patients, Freud came to understand "parsimonious" as the result of the unconscious equivalence of feces and money. Withholding my feces when someone wants me to give them becomes symbolized by withholding money. Once we understand that this is the first big struggle for control, it is not hard to see why this fixation can also take the form of rebelliousness, even a sadistic rebelliousness.

It is interesting to consider how the widespread use of the automatic washer-dryer and availability of disposable diapers have changed our culture. When I was a baby, diapers were laboriously washed in a primitive washing machine and dried on a clothesline (weather permitting). I can sympathize with my mother wanting to get me out of diapers just as soon as possible. Modern conveniences made toilet training much less urgent for the parents of the generation that became teenagers in the 1960s. That may be one reason many of us who were adults in the 1960s looked with horror on the dress, appearance, and cleanliness habits of the kids.

Phallic Period

Around the third year, children become very interested in the anatomical difference between the sexes. Casual observation, and probably memory of our own childhoods, confirms that this difference is a matter of considerable interest and concern to a child. Freud and his followers quickly discovered that it had been a major concern of their patients, one that had enduring consequences.

It is not only the difference between the sexes that engages children as they enter this period. It is also the enormous pleasure that stimulation of the penis and clitoris can bring. Stimulation of the other "erotogenic zones" was undoubtedly satisfying, and continues to be, but this new pleasure becomes primary. Since this is the time when the difference between the sexes assumes major importance, the fantasy of genital contact with another person begins to appear. By the age of about five the fantasy life of children is no longer primarily auto-erotic but is beginning to focus on another person. Who that other person is and how that fantasy works out will concern us at length in Chapter 4.

Parental Response

In this period parents have to deal with children learning the pleasures of stimulating their clitoris or penis. Parental response to this practice, which can vary from punishment and terrifying threats of dire consequences to totally ignoring it, can have lasting impact. One might learn that pleasure is bad; one might learn that sexual pleasure specifically is bad. This particular guilt seems more common and severe among boys. One might try to stop masturbating and repeatedly fail, coming to believe that he is weak-willed and thereby building up a large supply of guilt. At the other end of the continuum, one might learn that parents seem not to object to this sort of pleasure.

It was common 100 years ago to casually threaten a boy with castration. This presumably still happens, but probably less commonly. Many therapists believe a little boy develops a fear of castration on his own without the threat being specifically made. Certainly once he has seen that little girls don't have a penis, he may well infer that they did once and that they had it taken away. Even without that startling discovery it would not be a hard punishment to imagine. The anatomical form of the penis lends itself to the fantasy of castration. If, for example, the child is doing something forbidden with a hammer, the hammer will certainly be taken away from him. The next logical step wouldn't be hard to imagine.

Little girls can't be threatened in that particular way. They may fantasize that castration has already happened, but it can't be used as a threat or to instill a fear of future consequences. However, all children can be made to fear loss of love and approval. That may be the girl's equivalent of castration anxiety.

Children of both sexes may see the genital difference as a sign of male superiority and female inferiority. The way parents deal with this can accentuate this or go a long way toward softening it.

Phallic Fixation

Phallic fixation describes the child who makes the transition from auto-erotic primacy to interpersonal sexuality incompletely or not at all. The fixation can take a number of forms. The child may grow into a person for whom masturbation is the most satisfying form of sex. A phallically fixated boy may grow into a man who proudly and aggressively uses his penis to penetrate and dominate rather than make love. In all aspects of his life he may use his personality in the same way he uses his penis. He is apt to devalue women and take pride in his masculine superiority.

A phallically fixated girl may grow into a woman with a sense of inferiority, particularly in relation to men. She may consequently believe she must be passive and submissive to men. She may rebel and assume an aggressive "masculine" stance in the world. Like phallically fixated boys, she may devalue women. She may resent her mother, unconsciously believing her mother is responsible for her being deficient.

People who are particularly fond of sports cars, single-engine airplanes, and guns are apt to have at least a mild phallic fixation.

Serious phallic fixation interferes with sexual fulfillment. The person may be totally inhibited or may be able to perform the sex act only mechanically and without emotional contact.

Phallic fixation can arise primarily in two ways. First, a serious conflict over masturbation can produce such a fixation. In *Portrait of the Artist as a Young Man,* James Joyce gives a harrowing picture of Irish boys threatened with a horrible hell and the conflict into which that plunges them. Less dramatic conflicts occur commonly when a child or adolescent is taught that it is immoral or unhealthy to masturbate and finds himself helplessly addicted. (Girls seem less likely than boys to become intensely conflicted over masturbation.) Second, the child might be traumatized by the discovery of genital differences. The girl might believe that the lack of a penis means she is inferior. A boy, discovering that there are people without a penis, might become seriously frightened that this could happen to him. He might then become cautious and fearful or he might defend himself against this fear through aggressive phallic pride.

Latency Period

We encountered this period of massive sexual repression in Chapter 1. We will explore it more fully in Chapter 4.

Genital Period

Freud observed that although fantasies of sharing sexual pleasures begin and often flourish during the phallic period, it is really at puberty that these come into their own. He called this the genital period. Adolescents become specifically concerned with the relation of penis to vagina and the interpersonal implications of that relationship. This is the time of the full flowering of the Oedipus complex, the topic of Chapter 4. We will confine ourselves here to noting that in the pregenital stages there is no implication of progressing maturity. Except for the fact that the child is older in the anal period than in the oral, the progression from the oral to the anal period is not seen as a step toward maturity. To Freud, the big step toward growing up comes when the child moves from auto-eroticism to the fantasies and desires of shared sexual pleasures.

In our examination of the psychosexual stages we saw how fixation might occur at each stage. As we noted, one of the most important aspects of fixation is its relation to *regression*, responding to frustration or anxiety by returning to an earlier stage or relationship.

Regression Revisited

Freud described regression in this way: If something in later life inhibits the development of normal sexuality, the consequence may be the reappearance of an infantile form of sexuality. He compared this process to "a stream of water which meets with an obstacle in the river bed, is dammed up and flows back into old channels which had formerly seemed fated to run dry."[2] Regression thus means dealing with anxiety or frustration by retreating to an earlier psychosexual stage or an earlier relationship.

Originally this referred specifically to returning to an earlier sexual adjustment, but Freud's followers have expanded the concept. For example, regression now might include abandoning a stance of self-reliance for a previously discarded dependency or following a serious frustration with a return to a childish aggressiveness.

There is a strong relation between regression and fixation. The stronger the fixation at a given stage, the more likely it is that the frustrated or anxious person will regress to that stage.

Freud explained fixation and regression by use of this analogy: Consider a migrating tribe that, as it moves from place to place, leaves large detachments behind at some of its stopping places. If the advance parties run into trouble or encounter a dangerous enemy, they are likely to fall back to the places where they have left supporters. But if they have left too many people behind, they will be in more danger of being defeated should they run into opposition.[3] People who run into problems in love relationships sometimes retreat to the phallic period and discover that masturbation is safer and more satisfying than the complexities of interpersonal love. The pornography industry takes profitable advantage of this fact.

> Chet, a client of mine, very much wants to keep his present love affair alive. But as the usual complexities of a re-

lationship emerge, he is becoming so compulsively orderly and so rigidly insistent on things being done his way that he is in imminent danger of driving the woman away.

Frank, an adult client of a supervisee of mine, responded to a painful divorce by moving into his parents' house and almost literally clinging to his mother.

Serious fixation and regression are factors in neurosis, but milder instances appear in everyday life. I sometimes ask my students, "When you have a paper due tomorrow morning, what are you likely to do to postpone having to face it?" Some report that they fix themselves something to eat; some feel sure they cannot work on the paper until they have organized the desk or even cleaned the room. Myself a notorious phallic fixate, I tend to study gadget catalogues.

It is useful to remember that these are not random procrastinations. They are either meaningful retreats to a safer place or meaningful attempts to get out of trouble. As a child, my compulsive student was chastised or even punished for being messy. She learned, "When in trouble, clean up your act!" As she fears being unable to complete the paper on time, that old mantra emerges from the depths and she sets about to clean her room.

We might note in Freud's story of the migrating tribe that the group does not stop its migration when it leaves a detachment behind. It keeps on moving, although with depleted numbers and more vulnerability to attack. The implication is that fixation at a psychosexual stage does not so much stop the person from progressing to the next stage as it leaves the adult with less energy available for adult concerns.

From the point of view of psychosexual development, those adult concerns and adulthood itself begin at puberty. Now the adolescent is faced with the final challenge of the psychosexual journey: the Oedipus complex, which is the subject of Chapter 4.

4

THE OEDIPUS COMPLEX

Oedipus: Once on a time the oracle said that I should lie with my own mother and take on my hands the blood of my own father.
Jocasta: Before this in dreams too, . . . many a man has lain with his mother.

—Sophocles, *Oedipus Rex*

One of the many reasons Shakespeare's *Hamlet* has fascinated audiences and readers for 400 years is that Hamlet's motivations are so puzzling. Within the month following the death of Hamlet's father, his mother marries her dead husband's brother. Hamlet learns from his father's ghost that the uncle, now also his stepfather, had seduced his mother and murdered his father. He swears revenge and sets about plotting to kill his uncle. For five long, fascinating acts he delays, hesitates, vacillates, and rationalizes. We wonder, why is he so paralyzed? We know he's capable of action, even of murder. We've seen him unhesitatingly kill an old man who is spying on him. Why can't he just kill the villain and get it over with? That question has long occupied audiences, readers, and scholars.

Hamlet's behavior didn't seem so mysterious to Freud. The key to its interpretation, he argued, was the phenomenon that he called the Oedipus complex.

The most important aspect of the phallic period, that psychosexual stage that focuses our attention on the genitals, is its introduction of the Oedipus complex. Of all psychodynamic concepts, this may well be the most important to a clinician and the one that will most illuminate the inner lives of many of us. Freud said repeatedly that he considered it the centerpiece of his theory.

Freud introduced the concept of the Oedipus complex in *The Interpretation of Dreams,* first published in 1900:

> Being in love with the one parent and hating the other are among the essential constituents of the stock of psychical impulses which is formed [in childhood] and which [in children destined to grow up neurotic] is of such importance in determining their symptoms. This discovery is confirmed by a legend that has come down to us from classical antiquity: a legend whose profound and universal power to move can only be understood if the hypothesis I have put forward in regard to the psychology of children has an equally universal validity. What I have in mind is the legend of King Oedipus and Sophocles' drama which bears his name.[1]

In the drama to which Freud refers, Oedipus is the son of Laius and Jocasta, king and queen of the Greek city-state of Thebes. Laius is warned by an oracle that Oedipus will grow up to kill his father and marry his mother. To save himself Laius has his infant son left exposed on a mountain to perish. But Oedipus is saved by a shepherd. He is taken to another city, where he is adopted by the king and queen and grows up believing he is actually their son. He learns of the oracle and flees his adopted city, believing it is his adopted father who is in danger. On his travels he meets Laius and in a quarrel kills him. Then he saves Thebes from a terrible curse, is made king, and is given Jocasta, the widowed queen, to marry. When, at the end of the play, he learns that he has inadvertently killed his father and married his mother, he is overcome with horror, blinds himself, and leaves Thebes to become a wandering, homeless beggar.

Freud observed that the play has continued to have an impact on audiences for thousands of years. He believed that the drama's lasting power is the result of our unconscious recognition that Oedipus's story is ours, that the curse laid on him before his birth was also laid on each of us. Freud saw it as our destiny to go through a stage in which we would long for intimate connection with the parent of the opposite sex and suffer angry jealousy of our rival, the same-sex parent. Our subsequent mental health, he thought, depends in large part on our becoming able to relinquish those feelings, but few of us rid ourselves of them entirely. In most of us some part of them remain in the unconscious, and just as the horrified Oedipus finally discovers his guilt, Freud thought, we in the audience feel the impact of the powerful wishes and fears that lurk in our own unconscious.

Based on listening to the fantasies of his patients and revealed by his own self-analysis was Freud's belief that all boys experience the unconscious wish to get rid of father and replace him as mother's lover, and that all girls carry the unconscious wish to eliminate mother and replace her as father's lover. Because these fantasies are so dangerous and frightening, they are universally repressed; that is, they remain deeply buried in the person's unconscious. Buried though they are, they generate awesome conflicts and continue to wield a major influence on the person's life.

In our time, people who study psychoanalytic theory write or read a paragraph like the preceding one quite casually, as though there were nothing startling about its contents. Then, depending on their theoretical orientation, they may think, "Oh, yes, of course," or, "What bizarre nonsense." Whichever response is evoked, custom has dulled the impact of the theory of the Oedipus complex.

If the Oedipus theory is true, however, it, as much as the theory of the unconscious, requires a radical revision of common understanding of the human condition. It implies that the human being is born into a remarkable conflict. A graphic statement of this conflict comes from Gardner Lindzey, a social psychologist trained in behavior genetics. Lindzey reported the anthropological observation that one of the very few customs common to all societies is the incest taboo. He explained this by presenting the large body of evidence that inbreeding produces offspring significantly less well fitted for survival than does outbreeding, and that therefore only societies that forbade incest would have survived. Further, the *need* for a taboo implies that there is a very strong impulse that must be inhibited. "It seems unlikely that there would have been universal selection in favor of such a taboo if there were not . . . widespread impulses toward expression of the prohibited act. Cultures seldom focus upon the inhibition of behavior which few individuals feel compelled to display."[2] Lindzey argued that to reduce the centrality of the Oedipus complex, as many psychoanalytic revisionists do, is to deprive psychoanalytic theory of its central insight, however much it may improve the theory's public relations.

Since Freud first proposed this theory there has been widespread interest in the question of its universality. Even if overwhelming clinical evidence makes it clear that the Oedipus complex is common, if not universal, in our society, the question remains: Is it peculiar to our society or perhaps to our *type* of society, or is it universal?

The anthropologist Allen W. Johnson and the psychiatrist Douglass Price-Williams explored this question in *Oedipus Ubiquitous,* a major cross-cultural study of folktales. As the title suggests, they found that the Oedipus complex, at least as it applies to *boys,* was indeed universal, that is, found in folktales of every culture:

> We found little evidence that the motif of the men of the family fighting over the women of the family was a property only of tales told in stratified patriarchal societies. On the contrary, . . . the core tale of a boy who struggles to replace father as husband to his mother is remarkably widespread.
>
> Far from being diminished in strength the greater the distance from Freud's Vienna, the tale can actually be bolder in remote societies. . . . In these tales the actors do not accidentally commit murder and incest, but act willfully and without apparent guilt or remorse. Nonetheless, in most cases they are punished in some way. . . . In no human society are "oedipal crimes" taken lightly.[3]

Freud's critics have long argued that the Oedipus complex occurs only in male-dominated, class-structured societies; that it is a pathological consequence of such societies. Johnson and Price-Williams reported that the Oedipus complex turns up in the folktales of every culture they studied. The main distinction between the class-stratified societies like our own and the non-stratified societies is that in the latter the sexual and aggressive aspects of the Oedipal tales are significantly less disguised, that is, less repressed, than they are in societies like ours.

From their study the authors concluded that whether we follow Freud, who sees the Oedipal feelings as an inherited given whose genetic basis was laid in the millions of years it took for a divergent ape to evolve into a human being, or those who see it as the learned outcome of the child's socialization experiences, it seems apparent that Oedipal feelings are apt to arise in most children and color their emotional lives when they raise their own families.

Although the folktale evidence supports the Oedipal hypothesis as it affects *boys,* the authors did not find the same evidence about girls:

> The girl's oedipal situation, as viewed through world folk literature, is significantly different from that imagined by Freud. Whereas in the boy's oedipal situation we follow . . . Freud in emphasizing the mutual mother-son eroticism and the mutual father-son hostility, in the girl's case we found father most often initiated incestuous actions toward daughter: daughter as a rule did not reciprocate father's interest and did not see mother as a competitor.[4]

The authors added that they did find a smaller number of tales portraying the daughter as the sexual aggressor toward the father, and inferred that in unconscious relations between family members erotic or hostile feelings are rarely unilateral. However, taken with the preponderance of brother-sister tales in which the brother is the sexual aggressor, they reported that there is overall a tendency for men to be seen as the sexually interested partners, whereas women are portrayed as opposed, indifferent, or passively acquiescent.

It may well be that one of the basic truths revealed by this study is that, at least where incest is concerned, males are much more desirous and assertive than females. However, there is another possibility: We will see later in this chapter psychoanalyst Jessica Benjamin's proposal that males of Western culture (possibly of all cultures?) are motivated to deny that females can have sexual desire. There is clinical evidence for that hypothesis as well as a good deal of logic behind it. The literature of our culture, and many other cultures as well, is full of references to the masculine fear of being betrayed by an unfaithful woman. In Shakespeare's plays, for example, a common response to hearing that a male friend is engaged is jokes about the impending, inevitable betrayal. This is presumably less threatening if all the husband has to fear is the lust of other men. If he also has to fear the lust of his wife, the danger is multiplied. Perhaps it's possible that the pattern observed in these folktales represents a species-wide defense against the fear of desire, at least of incestuous desire, in females.

There is a great deal of clinical evidence that, in our culture at least, girls experience the Oedipus complex. There are significant differences from how it affects boys; we will look at those in some detail.

Johnson and Price-Williams noted that few of us acknowledge openly to ourselves or others the common heritage we share of ambivalent feelings toward our most intimate relatives. They conclude that even exceptionally introspective people, including those who can intellectually accept the universality of incestuous and aggressive impulses in families, have difficulty detecting any such feelings in themselves:

> To us, this suggests the enormous importance to humankind of control over impulsive behavior that could shatter the nuclear family, and still larger social units upon which our basic existence depends. Evidently, so dangerous are the erotic and aggressive impulses that even to admit they exist is prohibited.[5]

Since Freud first described the Oedipus complex, psychoanalysts have placed increasing importance on the way that parents deal with it in their children. Some (Heinz Kohut, for example) have gone so far as to argue that since it is the combination of parental seduction and threat, however subtle, that makes the Oedipus complex so fraught with problems for the adolescent, the Oedipal period can be essentially problem-free if the parents have been loving and sensitive throughout the adolescent's life. Few analysts have gone that far, most believing that it's nearly impossible to be *that* sensitive. It means skating through one dilemma after another. For example, it's not easy to affirm enthusiastically the adolescent's blooming sexuality without being seductive. Most analysts now hold the position that the Oedipus complex and its resolution are fraught with psychological difficulties for the child under the best of circumstances, but that those difficulties can certainly be made much easier or more difficult by the parental response.

When Freud first began treating women with neurotic problems, he was struck by the frequency with which they told stories of childhood sexual encounters with an adult, often their father. He developed the theory that these early sexual experiences predisposed a child to later neurosis. It seemed to him a major discovery, one that he hoped might bring him much-desired fame. Gradually and reluctantly he began to discover that the situations described in some of the stories could not possibly be true, and he began to suspect that some of the stories were fantasies. It was some years before he could bring himself to publish this discovery. However much this damaged his first theory, it was a major advance in our understanding of the mind; it was the beginning of our recognition that fantasy carries a remarkable power and that there is some place in the mind where fantasy and reality lack a clear boundary; it was the beginning of the discovery of primary process and of repression.

In the 1980s and 1990s much was written about this understanding, and there has been a good deal of controversy about it. Jeffery Masson's *Assault on Truth*[6] claimed that political cowardice caused Freud to abandon the theory that neurosis was caused by an adult seducing a child: the "seduction theory." However, the truth is that Freud believed to the end of his life that sexual abuse of children was more prevalent than had been previously believed and that such abuse was disastrous for the child. He also believed it was possible for a child to confuse the fantasy of desired sex with the reality. Masson accused Freud of cowardice, but at the time Freud's new theory of sexual desire in children was probably even more politically dangerous than the seduction theory. It seems that nineteenth-century Viennese doctors were more ready to believe that some men were scoundrels than to believe that their own children harbored sexual desires and impulses.

As a result of this highly visible controversy, some people now believe that all emotional troubles stem from early sexual abuse, even if the person doesn't remember it. It is certainly true that some costly instances of sexual abuse are repressed, and uncovering them is often therapeutic. But the belief that sexual abuse is the cause of *all* emotional problems has had some untoward consequences; a therapist convinced that this is the primary issue for all clients can make it very difficult for those clients to resist obligingly "remembering" such a history. As a result, some innocent parents and childcare workers have been placed in real jeopardy.[7]

There is undoubtedly a distressing incidence of actual child abuse. It also seems likely that there are considerably more instances of *subtle* seduction stemming from the parental unconscious. Such subtle seduction can also be a problem. It can be very confusing to a child as it meshes with the child's unconscious wishes. It's not hard to see how the hazards of the Oedipus complex can be increased or reduced by parental response.

There are three major implications of Freud's Oedipal theory:

1. The theory of the Oedipus complex tells us (and particularly tells the clinician) something crucial about our unconscious mental life.
2. The phenomena described by this theory are an inevitable part of the human condition. This includes the attitudes of men and women toward themselves and each other. In Freud's view that meant male assertiveness and female seductive passivity.
3. All things considered, Freud thought that male assertiveness and female seductive passivity were probably the best arrangement.

All three of these implications have been sharply and repeatedly criticized. Psychoanalytic revisionists have challenged the very existence of the Oedipus complex. Many critics, particularly feminist psychoanalysts, although accepting the existence of the Oedipus complex and refining its conceptualization, have persuasively argued that the form it takes in our culture is in large part the product of that culture and by no means inevitable. These same critics have been the most articulate in pointing out the sexism of the third implication.

We will, in this account, follow the feminist psychoanalysts in taking the position that, however flawed the first two implications are, for good or ill the theory of the Oedipus complex tells us something absolutely crucial about our unconscious mental life, and a clinician working without a grasp of this theory is seriously handicapped.

For almost 50 years Freud worked at refining and clarifying the Oedipal theory. Similarly, his colleagues and followers have worked on it energetically. There is probably no account of the development of the Oedipus complex about which every theorist would agree. The following account may be as uncontroversial as any, and it seems most useful to me. It owes a good deal to the work of feminist psychoanalysts Jessica Benjamin[8] and Nancy Chodorow.[9]

We begin by observing certain aspects of our society:

1. Women are the first important parent. Because women give birth and provide milk, this is unlikely to change. So, perhaps forever, most children experience mother as the first caretaker and also as soft, cuddly, and protective.

2. Men occupy a world outside the home. Father is likely to represent that outside world. He is also likely to be playful rather than soft and cuddly, and to be physically more powerful.

3. We continue to live in a man's world. Men have authority and are expected to dominate. Jessica Benjamin believes that patriarchy is so deeply embedded in the culture that excising it from the culture's collective unconscious will not happen overnight. Therefore, no matter how much enlightened parents may soften the message for a given child, and she thinks it crucial that they do, for years to come it will still be true that the unconscious of children in this culture will be imprinted with the message of male dominance. Benjamin is not without optimism. She has glimpsed a new world in the unmistakable movement toward gender equality.

Mother is the first caretaker for both boys and girls. This establishes a powerful bond, probably one that is never really broken. But this bond has a frightening aspect for the child: Relative to the helpless child, mother is overwhelmingly powerful, and the child's prospects of developing individuality and autonomy may be significantly threatened by the power of the mother. In the psychoanalytic vocabulary the conflict between security and autonomy has come to be known as the *rapprochement* conflict.

The origins of this concept are interesting and relevant to our present inquiry. Margaret Mahler, who began her career as a pediatrician in Vienna and emigrated to the United States in the 1930s, was one of the most important psychoanalytic observers of infants and their development.[10] She observed that in the second year of life the toddler encounters a severe conflict between dependency and autonomy. On the one hand the child wants contact with mother and also her protection. On the other hand there is a vast new world to be explored and the child yearns to feel powerful and free. There are more or less benign solutions to this conflict, but conflict it is, and one that teaches lasting lessons. Mahler observed that the mother who can lovingly support the child's alternating impulses in both directions is most apt to help the child minimize the subsequent conflict between abandonment and engulfment, although perhaps no one escapes it entirely. Mahler named this period *rapprochement* (reconciliation) because in the previous developmental stage the child had shown less interest in maternal contact, often leading mother to feel abandoned. During the rapprochement stage the child returns to a desire for closeness with mother, a *reconciliation*, although as we have seen above, this rapprochement is intermittent.

Enter father. From the beginning, through the rapprochement phase, father has played a less important role in this drama. Typically he has not been around as much as mother. Also typically he represents the outside world with all its fascinating freedom. He seems more powerful than mother. He is physically stronger and he is masculine in a world that ascribes dominance to masculinity. Recall that mother's power, vastly superior to that of the child, has been and continues to be frightening and inhibiting. As father's role in the drama becomes significant, there appears a way to neutralize mother's power: a connection with father.

The drama is now different for boys and girls. Boys know they are like father in one significant respect not shared by mother or sister: They have a penis. Conversely, girls realize that the absence of a penis is a visible difference from father. Freud made much of this childhood discovery. He believed that both boys and girls thought that anyone without a penis was incomplete and inferior. He further believed that a child's most likely supposition was that the girl had once had a penis but had lost it. In Freud's view, this made castration seem a realistic danger to boys. It also burdened girls with a lifelong "penis envy," an envy that shaped much of their subsequent psychology. Freud's understanding of these phenomena was undoubtedly shaped by his beliefs in male superiority and the intrinsic superiority of everything masculine, including the penis. Because some of his prejudices are quite evident, it is tempting to disregard his theories about the importance of the penis, and indeed early feminist critics did just that. However, some prominent contemporary feminist psychoanalysts recognized that elements of these theories are clinically indispensable and they set about reexamining the phenomenon.

Let's look first the development of the Oedipus complex in boys. To the little boy, at around the age of five father appears as a hopeful antidote to mother's frightening power. Father is as powerful as mother, maybe more powerful; identifying with him provides the boy with a sense of his own power. And it is indeed significant that father has a penis. That's what distinguishes him from mother, and the penis is an important sign of the similarity of father and son. The penis becomes a symbol of father's power, of the son's eventual power, and of the power of masculinity. The boy identifies with his father, thus protecting himself from mother's power. He is male; he is complete. Father welcomes him, recognizing himself as a boy and thus identifying with him. A masculine comradeship is established.

Although the boy flees the frightening power of his mother, she is still his first love. As he identifies with father, and as he perceives the importance of the penis, this love takes on a new form, erotic desire. In addition to his loving identification with father, he now finds in him a rival for this new form of his love for mother, giving rise in the boy to resentment and hostility. This is the Oedipus complex in boys: The early attachment to mother has taken on an important erotic aspect, and his father, still loved at some level of consciousness, has become a rival. Rivalry with such a powerful figure is dangerous, and thus to this complicated set of emotions toward the father, another is added: fear. Actually, a *pair* of emotions is added: fear and guilt. The inevitable course of the boy's unconscious life has brought him into sharp, painful conflict with two of the most forbidden of all desires, incest and patricide. As discussed in Chapter 2, primary process thought does not make fine distinctions between gently replacing the father and killing him. When we consider the *resolution* of the Oedipus complex, we will see that one of the most crucial tasks for the adolescent is coming to terms with that fear and guilt.

The attachment to mother and the rivalry with father is very likely to be abetted by the parents. For reasons we will consider shortly, the mother's attachment to her baby son is itself likely to be erotic and seductive, however subtly. Men sometimes joke about having lost their wives to their infant sons. Often this is more than a joke. For some women this is the male they have been waiting for. This is a conflict-free love affair, one in which they are in complete control. Because it is erotic without being consummated, it satisfies whatever sex-guilt they carry.

Although father has identified with his son and welcomed him as a new little comrade, his feelings are actually extremely ambivalent. Here is a dramatic manifestation of the generation that will replace him. Here is youth and unlimited potential, providing a disturbing contrast to his own recognition of aging and mortality. Also, it must be acknowledged, many men find it irresistible to confront a male whom they can dominate so completely. But above all, the son is now a rival for the wife's love, and father finds himself feeling competitive and sometimes even hostile. Let's recall how the Oedipus story begins. Oedipus has not knowingly committed a crime. The crime committed in full awareness was not that of Oedipus but that of Laius, who tried to murder his innocent infant son. It has thus often been suggested that the complex should be called the Laius complex.

Hostility of father toward son and fathers' suspicion of apparently innocent sons are dominant themes in the life and literature of our culture. In Shakespeare, when Macbeth kills Duncan, king of Scotland, Duncan's sons take for granted they will be accused of the crime and flee. Henry IV accuses Hal, his loyal and loving son, of being impatient for his death so he, Hal, can ascend the throne. Most therapists report that it is a rare male client who felt loved and supported by his father. One client of mine recalled being taught to box by his father when he was about 10 years old. Following instructions to try to hit his father, he landed a lucky punch and his father promptly knocked him to the ground. His enraged father stood over him and said, "Don't ever do anything like that to me again." This story is a bit more dramatic than most, but the theme is almost ubiquitous.

Research by the anthropologist John Whiting throws light on the phenomenon of father's hostile rivalry toward his son.[11] In some polygamous cultures mothers and babies sleep together for the first year of the baby's life. The father is excluded from this bed. These societies practice initiation rites for pubescent boys that are more severe than in other cultures. The adult men, including the boy's father, initiate him into the men's world by subjecting him to considerable pain, often involving genital mutilation. It is not hard to imagine the unconscious forces that cause a father whose son has effectively pushed him out of his wife's bed to perform a symbolic castration when the boy reaches puberty.

We turn now to the development of the Oedipus complex in girls. This involves a particular complication. Whereas the boy's Oedipal love object is the same person he has loved and needed from the beginning, typically the girl shifts from her mother, the initial attachment, to a new love object, her father.

Like her brother, the young girl needs an antidote to mother's overwhelming power. Like him, she needs help in establishing her independence from mother. Also like him she turns to father, and here she meets disappointment. She cannot identify with father as her brother can. She is all too aware of the significant physiological difference: She has no penis. Typically father does not welcome her as a little comrade the way he does the boy. He is more apt to treat her as an adorable, seductive little person. She learns the first painful consequence of not having a penis: She is excluded from identification and comradeship with her powerful father, who could protect her from her overwhelmingly powerful mother, and who could champion the cause of her autonomy and individuation.

If he won't accept her as a comrade, if she is not equipped to be her father's comrade, how *might* she recruit him to help her break free from mother? There are clues: Mother's love for him is erotic, and the girl is still strongly identified with mother. Father treats her as adorable and seductive. Although she has no penis, as his lover she can possess his and thereby partake of his power. Thus occurs the shift from mother to father as her primary love object.

Her relationship with mother now becomes extremely complicated. Mother is her first love and the person with whom the girl identifies. But now mother is her rival for father's love. This is the Oedipus complex in girls: erotic desire for father coupled with a confusing, ambivalent, angry rivalry with mother. Because of her power, mother has always been feared as well as loved, and now the girl has new reason for that fear. Like the little boy, she now has cause for severe unconscious guilt.

We have described the similarities in the Oedipal development of boys and girls. Both fear the overwhelming power of mother and both turn to father for protection. Both end by desiring the opposite-sex parent and seeing the same-sex parent as a rival. And we have seen the differences: The boy depends for protection on his similarity to father, the girl on her attractiveness. The boy ends by desiring the parent he has always loved and depended on; the girl must make the transition from loving mother to loving and desiring father.

We now come to a chapter in the child's development that is crucial for her or his future: the resolution of the Oedipus complex. At this point in our story the child is in a critically untenable position. If a girl, there is no way she can replace mother as father's lover without disastrous results. Her task now is to extricate herself from this untenable position in a way that gives her the best possible chance for a healthy adolescence and adulthood. This means the best possible sexual adjustment, but it is by no means limited to that. How she resolves the Oedipus complex will affect the extent to which she can joyfully accept herself as a woman, and it will have a major impact on her relationships with men and women.

It must be said that the path toward resolution is strewn with pitfalls for both boys and girls. The girl may emerge feeling guilty about sex or about her relationships with older women. She may find herself in conflict about her sexual identity. She may find her love life seriously hampered by an inability to feel passionate and tender toward the same person. The boy faces the same task and the same pitfalls, although, as we will see, there are differences. It may be that no one gets through this developmental crisis without some scars and without some lasting burden. Sensitive and loving parents can minimize the burden but probably not eliminate it.

Freud thought that the Oedipus complex developed in two stages. The first appears during the phallic period. It is this first stage that we have been exploring above, and it is here that the resolution of the Oedipus complex begins. The second Oedipal stage follows puberty, and it is there that the resolution finally flowers. In between those two Oedipal stages is the stage Freud labeled "Latency."

Latency Period

This period lasts from about the age of six until puberty. The erotic impulses of the phallic period are repressed, as is the Oedipus complex. Freud thought that for most children all sexuality is repressed during this period. He thought both socialization and the course of instinctual development contributed to this. It seems likely that the terror of incestuous fantasies is a major contributor to the repression that begins the latency period. Freud acknowledged, however, that many children continue to experience powerful sexual impulses during this period. In our culture these impulses express themselves as masturbation, but in cultures where it is permitted, childhood sexual activity, including intercourse, is common in the years before puberty. Whereas the incest taboo and the Oedipus complex appear to be universal phenomena, it seems that the latency period is culture-specific. There is, however, little evidence bearing on whether, even in permissive cultures, the Oedipus complex is repressed during those years.

The latency period was of particular importance in Freud's view because he thought it contributed to the human vulnerability to neurosis. He reasoned that sensuality, including Oedipal sensuality, finds its greatest development in the phallic period. Then, that sensuality meets opposition, often in the form of socialization. The child may feel guilt or shame or even disgust, and sensuality is repressed. When a sudden flood of hormones into the system breaks through the repression barrier and ends the latency period, it brings awareness of sensuality back in full force. The danger is that the repression that ushered in the latency period may leave scars. The adolescent now begins to confront what may be the hardest of developmental problems. He or she must bring the sensual currents of his or her impulses into harmony with the tender, loving impulses. It is a severe psychological burden not to be able to love whom we desire and not to be able to desire whom we love. And it is distressingly common. Freud wondered if anyone escapes it altogether. He thought that accomplishing this harmony was made much harder by the advent of the latency period. Had sexuality been permitted to develop unimpeded, had a massive repression not intervened, the smooth development of a healthy adult sexuality in which love and desire are harmonized would have been more likely.

The Genital Period: Resolving the Oedipus Complex

As the onslaught of hormones propels pubescent children into adolescence, they enter what Freud called the *genital period,* in which they are faced with the crucial task of resolving the Oedipus complex. It is likely that the seeds of the resolution had been sown in the phallic period, and now they flower. As we have noted, how the Oedipus complex is resolved will determine a great deal about how the pubescent child will go on to deal with adolescent and adult sexuality.

Resolution of the Oedipus complex can take many forms, but one thing appears to be universal: To a large extent adolescents must liberate themselves from their erotic attachment to the parent and find a way to direct that energy toward appropriate new people. A healthy adjustment requires relating to these new people in a way that is not burdened by an unconscious fixation on the parent.

It is not easy to make the transition from the Oedipal object of desire, but it is made less difficult by sensitive cooperation from the parents. Fathers face the delicate task of lovingly affirming their daughters' attractive femininity without being seductive. Mothers face the analogous task with their sons. It is very important that sons not sense they are more attractive and interesting to mother than is father, and that girls not sense they are more attractive and interesting to father than is mother.

Freud thought the ideal resolution of the Oedipus complex (seldom completely achieved) would lead to a heterosexual adjustment in which the adolescent/adult could experience tender and passionate feelings toward the same person, where he or she could love whom he or she desires and desire whom he or she loves.*

Freud would not have been surprised by recent research suggesting that some homosexuals appear to have been born with a powerful predisposition to homosexuality and are very likely to make that choice, whatever their childhood experiences. He believed that to some extent we are all bisexual, but that there are marked individual differences in the balance of our heterosexual and homosexual predispositions.

To achieve completely the goal of the successful joining of tenderness and passion, Freud thought the Oedipus complex had to be abolished—not just repressed, but totally destroyed. If it were repressed it would continue to wield a destructive influence, whereas if it were abolished, meaning that it didn't even exist in the unconscious, the person would be freed to enjoy a satisfying adult sexuality. It is doubtful that Freud or any of his followers believed the complex was ever completely abolished, desirable though that goal might be. In theory he

---

*A word is in order about Freud's belief that a heterosexual adjustment was ideal. Considering the time and culture in which he worked, Freud had amazingly little homophobia. There is a famous incident in which an American woman wrote him asking if psychoanalysis could cure her son's homosexuality. Following is an excerpt of his reply, written in 1935: Dear Mrs. . . .

I gather from your letter that your son is a homosexual. I am most impressed by the fact that you do not mention this term yourself in your information about him. May I question you why you avoid it? Homosexuality is assuredly no advantage, but it is nothing to be ashamed of, no vice, no degradation; it cannot be classified as an illness; we consider it to be a variation of the sexual function, produced by a certain arrest of sexual development. Many highly respectable individuals of ancient and modern times have been homosexuals, several of the greatest men among them. (Plato, Michelangelo, Leonardo da Vinci etc.) It is a great injustice to persecute homosexuality as a crime—and a cruelty, too. If you do not believe me, read the books of Havelock Ellis. . . .

thought that it was more likely to be abolished in boys than in girls because of the powerful fear of castration.

The "Positive" Resolution

To achieve the goal of a satisfying, well-adjusted heterosexual life, the adolescent boy comes to identify with his father and thus abandons the dangerous, competitive struggle. He determines (unconsciously) to find a girl like father found, that is, a girl like mother. However, the competition having been abandoned and the incest taboo accepted, it is clear that mother herself is not eligible.

Similarly, the adolescent girl comes to identify with mother, abandons the competitive struggle, and sets out to find a man like father. Freud called this the "positive" resolution and thought it offered the best hope for a well-adjusted adulthood. He also thought that it seldom, if ever, worked out so well that the adolescent was completely untroubled by the Oedipus complex.

The "Negative" Resolution

In his early writings on the Oedipus complex, Freud described the "negative" resolution as one in which the adolescent renounces the competition by adopting the homosexual position. This can come about in a number of ways. Freud describes a patient who longed to have a baby from her father. At the height of this longing her mother became pregnant. The girl felt betrayed, furious that her father had given her mother the baby she so wanted. In her rage she turned away not only from her father but from all men. She became exclusively homosexual. Thereafter she had ambivalent feelings toward her mother, an ambivalence that included a good deal of competitive hostility. She felt guilty and distressed by these feelings because she also retained much of her early childhood attachment to her mother. She dealt with this guilt by symbolically taking her mother as the object of desire and falling in love with a woman who reminded her of her mother. Also, her mother avidly sought the attention of men, and by becoming homosexual the daughter abandoned that field to her mother, thus avoiding competition with her on this score.

This case of Freud's contains one of his most important and valuable insights, that a common response to loss is to identify with the lost person, to take him or her or some important part of that person into oneself, thus psychically undoing the loss. Freud had described this phenomenon in a paper on mourning, and here he shows how it reinforced his patient's homosexual solution: She had lost her father, and now in some sense she became him by also becoming one who loves women.

> A male client of mine came to see me because he was disturbed by occasional homosexual urges. He thought of himself as heterosexual, had had only heterosexual experiences, and was married with children. His heterosexual life had always been markedly unsatisfactory and continued to be. Every once in a while he would have an irresistible urge to seek a homosexual partner. He would go out and wander through a section of town known to be a pick-up district for men. He was afraid to pick anyone up and never responded to overtures, but he obtained some satisfaction by just cruising the streets. And then he would be assailed by strong feelings of shame.

From as early in life as he could remember, his father was a flagrant philanderer, seldom home. The father made no attempt to hide his infidelities. My client recalled always longing for contact with him. As we worked together, we learned that he had grown up believing that his father was only interested in sex and the women who provided it. Eventually he came to believe unconsciously that his father would love him if he could provide that sex. He wandered the streets unconsciously hoping to pick up his father.

The Tenderness/Passion Split

Freud believed, as we have seen, that a crucial and difficult task in the development of a person's sexuality is bringing the sensual currents of his or her impulses into harmony with the tender, loving impulses. He suspected that no one manages to do this completely, and his practice taught him that many people suffer greatly from this split between their tender and their sensual impulses. Popular culture knows this as the Madonna-and-the-whore phenomenon, although it certainly occurs in women as well.

The Oedipal explanation is that the incest taboo forbids passionate feelings toward a parent. I may have *tender* feelings toward my mother; in fact it is expected that I will have them. But I must repress my passionate feelings toward her. The same phenomenon pertains to a girl and her father. So when I grow up and seek a woman to love, to the extent that this conflict has a hold on me, I am really seeking *two* women, or perhaps two *types* of women. I meet women "like mother" toward whom I feel tender and loving and whom I will introduce to my parents and whom I may very well marry. If, because of the incest taboo, I find my passionate impulses more or less severely curtailed with these "nice" or "virtuous" or "cultured" women, I also seek out women I categorize quite differently with whom to share passion. It was well known in the ante-bellum South that young upper-class men dated and married the debutantes but had sex in the slave cabins. This still goes on: At the university in the Southwest where I taught, the fraternity boys dated (and presumably married) the sorority girls, but for sex they crossed the border. It is sad to imagine the married sex life of those "nice" girls. Among many other people, although this tenderness-passion split manifests itself more subtly, it remains a distressing problem.

The Oedipal Victor

We noted previously, that parents can facilitate or hinder a successful resolution of the Oedipus complex. One of the most common and destructive outcomes of the complex is that in which the child believes he or she has won the competition with the same-sex parent. There are a number of ways in which this can come about for girls and boys.

For a girl to consider herself the Oedipal victor she must get the message either that her mother has abdicated in her favor or that her father simply prefers her to her mother. That preference may be sexual, even without actual abuse. The father may see in his daughter the young, vibrant wife he married and send a clear message of sensual attraction. Or he may find his daughter a better companion or a more sympathetic listener.

The mother may vacate the field in several ways. The most basic is for her to die while the daughter is still a child or adolescent. Unless the father is very sensitive, the daughter may find herself suddenly promoted to wife. There may be a divorce in which the daughter is left with the father. Or the mother may simply lose interest in the father and send the message that she would like the daughter to take over for her.

It is important to remember that these scenarios occur in the context of the Oedipus complex, which means that unconsciously the daughter passionately desires the victory. That is the reason the victory is so terribly costly. We recall once again that in the realm of primary process the wish is equivalent to the act: "I wanted to take him away from her and I have done it." Now the daughter unconsciously believes that she has willfully committed what may be the two most terrible sins: incest and matricide. She is certainly better off if the incest has been only symbolic, but psychic incest and matricide it is nevertheless, making her prey to consuming guilt.

Girls who see themselves as the Oedipal victor tend to grow up with a guilty fear of women, particularly older women. Unconsciously, they believe that they have willfully stolen from their mother and that some older woman will take revenge. Their relations with men are apt to be inhibited by the guilt deriving from their belief that they seduced their father into symbolic (or even actual) incest. We cannot remind ourselves too often that, in the realm of primary process, the wish is equivalent to the act.

A father sexually exploiting his daughter is a catastrophic betrayal for a number of obvious reasons. A reason not so apparent, but terribly costly, is that the child cannot be sure she did not bring it about through her Oedipal wish. The ensuing confusion and guilt are likely to be overwhelming.

> Marianna, a client who had been repeatedly sexually molested by her father, accompanied her husband to a party at the home of his boss, a woman some 20 years older than Marianna. After being introduced to her hostess she experienced a severe panic attack and had to ask her husband to take her away without delay. She told her therapist that, although she knew full well it was outlandish, she was convinced the hostess hated her and wanted to harm her.

Boys, of course, can be Oedipal victors also.

> Geoffrey consulted a therapist for a number of problems, including a distressing sexual inhibition with his wife. They were both in their mid-thirties and had had a satisfactory sexual relationship with each other before they married. When Geoffrey entered therapy they had been married for over a year, and their sexual relationship had been steadily deteriorating. In an early session Geoffrey revealed with some bewilderment that he had had a very difficult time bringing himself to kiss his wife at their wedding and had actually managed to find a way not to. It was some months later that he suddenly realized that had he kissed her at the wedding it would have been the first time he had kissed her in front of his mother.
>
> Geoffrey's parents had divorced when he was 10 years old. His mother never remarried or even dated. "You're my little man now," she told her son. Indeed she treated him that way. A couple of years later Geoffrey began regularly masturbat-

ing. He would masturbate in bed and ejaculate onto the bed sheet, making no attempt to conceal it. Each morning his mother would take the sheet off the bed, wash it, and replace it without comment. Geoffrey had no doubt that she was aware of the ejaculate. "We were actually making love, weren't we?" he said to his therapist.

One has to feel for Geoffrey's mother. She was left a young and lonely single mother. It's understandable that she turned to her beloved son to meet many of her needs. Nevertheless, this behavior left Geoffrey with serious impediments to his liberation from the Oedipus complex.

The divorce itself, actually removing his father from the scene, presented Geoffrey with real danger, however sensitively his mother had dealt with it. We have seen how crucial it is that children do not become convinced they have won the Oedipal struggle, and how important it is that parents maintain a constant position that there is no possibility of the child winning. Geoffrey *wanted* his father to disappear, and when his father actually left, Geoffrey unconsciously believed that his wish had been granted, that it was his fault his father left, in fact that he had murdered his father. In the realm of primary process the wish, for example the wish to kill, is equivalent to the act, and exile is equivalent to murder. Geoffrey would have believed that he had brought about his father's exile even if he had loved his father and had been consciously devastated by the divorce. Actually, however, he didn't like his father very much. He feared him and was relieved when he left.

This is not to imply that every child whose parents divorce around the time of the Oedipus complex becomes the Oedipal victor, with all the attendant dangers. Sensitive parents can make it clear to the child that the divorce does not imply that. Nevertheless, it's still difficult for the Oedipal child not to believe he or she caused the divorce.

The Consequences of the Oedipus Complex

The ultimate importance of the Oedipus complex is not that it gives the adolescent a few troubling years, but that it has lasting consequences, some extremely problematic. The rare individuals who emerge unscathed, necessarily with the help of extremely healthy and sensitive parents, go on to find a mate toward whom they can feel both tenderness and passion. Their relationships with both men and women are free of excessive guilt or fear, and they are able to raise their children with the same enlightened sensitivity with which they were raised. The rest of us deal with the Oedipal burden as best we can. Its intensity can vary from mild to crippling. We have already seen how it can keep us from loving and desiring the same person. It can have other consequences as well. To the extent that we are fixated on the desired parent, it can keep us from fully giving ourselves to a mate; we are committed elsewhere, perhaps like Don Juan going from woman to woman, unconsciously and futilely searching for his mother.

The Oedipus complex seems to have at its disposal no small number of ways to interfere with one's life. One of my very sophisticated clients, himself a therapist, used to ask me, "Am I afraid to approach this woman because she *is* my mother or because she *isn't*?" What he meant was that if the woman reminded him too much of his mother, the incest taboo would strike, but if she *didn't* sufficiently remind him of his mother, like Don Juan, his mother-fixation would cause him to move on, still searching.

> I once worked with a couple who had shared quite a satis-
> factory sex life at the beginning of their relationship. But
> as the relationship developed, the man became less and
> less available sexually. He rationalized this change by say-
> ing, and completely believing, that he had just become too
> busy. It eventually became clear that when his lover was a
> "date" he could permit himself to be excited by her, but as
> he began to anticipate her becoming *wife* and *mother*, the
> incest taboo struck. In addition, he had a persistent
> mother-fixation. My sophisticated client would have said,
> "He can't make love to her because she *is* his mother *and*
> because she *isn't*.

Although there are a number of similarities in how children of each sex attempt to reach resolution of the Oedipus complex, it is important to note that such resolution involves some issues unique to girls and some unique to boys.

The attachment between mother and her babies is typically much more intense than between father and the babies. Nancy Chodorow observes that this difference in the intensity of parental attachment continues as the children grow, that is, mother-love is likely to remain more intense than father-love.[12] Thus there are two factors at work, making the boy's Oedipus complex more intense than the girl's. His Oedipal love object is his first love, with all the power that implies. In addition, since mother-love is likely to be more intense than father-love, his Oedipal attachment is apt to be more strongly reciprocated than his sister's. Because it is more intense it will be more frightening and more resisted. It is particularly frightening because possession of the penis carries with it the danger that punishment for daring to be father's rival could be castration.

The girl is apt to relinquish the Oedipus complex more slowly and less completely. She will need to struggle against her love for father less energetically than the boy struggles against his love for mother.

One of Freud's most compelling insights is that one's identity is connected to the Oedipal resolution. We have seen that the daughter has identified with her mother from the beginning, and that the son has early identified with his father as a way of escaping the feared power of his mother. When the Oedipus complex turns the parent into a dangerous rival, the child discovers that intensifying the identification will provide protection. Psychoanalysis describes this phenomenon as "identification with the aggressor." At the time of Oedipal resolution this identification takes several forms.

Let's look first at the boy. One of the most important forms of the identification is that the boy *internalizes* his father's prohibition against erotic desire for his mother. It is no longer father saying, "Thou shalt not . . ." but the boy's own conscience, his superego. Freud pointed out what an interesting and adaptive form of protection this is. The danger is external. Father might punish or even castrate. In the world of secondary process there is no way to neutralize father; he's much more powerful than I. But what if I protect myself where I *do* have power, inside my own head? So I institute an effective prohibition against the dangerous wish, the wish that would get me punished if acted upon.

So far, so good. I am secure in my masculinity because of my identification with father, and I am protected from castration as long as I keep the incest wishes well buried. But there's a problem: I began my identification journey by loving and identifying with mother. To some extent that must have been fixating, and so there is always the danger of regressing to that feminine identification. Because the very early love was so closely connected to identification, there is every chance that my Oedipal love will stir those echoes. Identifying with a woman threatens my masculinity, giving rise to the fears held by so many males of softness and vulnerability. This analysis also helps us understand the widespread fear, even hatred, of homosexuals. It is not only my masculinity that is threatened. In that first love I was merged with my mother and thoroughly dependent on her. Any adolescent or adult echo of that love and that identification threatens my independence and autonomy as well.

Let's look now at the issues faced by girls as they attempt to resolve their Oedipus complex. Girls are not as motivated to destroy the Oedipus complex as are boys, partly because they are not under the threat of castration and partly because, to an adolescent, mother does not seem as dangerous as father. It therefore may be less threatening to a girl to love her father and seek a mate who resembles him.

However, like her brother, she began by loving and identifying with her mother. As she resolves the Oedipus complex she will strengthen that identification with her mother. One's first love is very compelling; that is why the Oedipus complex is so strong in boys. But in a girl the power of that first love competes with her heterosexual adjustment; the first love is a woman. As her identification with mother strengthens in the Oedipal resolution, so does her love for mother. This puts her in a very confusing position, one composed of a pair of conflicts. She is very likely to feel considerable anger and fear toward her Oedipal rival, yet this is the person who was her first love. That is the first conflict. The other conflict has to do with the heterosexual adjustment with which she is resolving the Oedipus complex. From a psychodynamic point of view, all love has an erotic component; strong love has a strong erotic component. The girl emerges from the Oedipus complex with residual erotic attachments to both mother and father. This helps us understand why heterosexual women thrive on tender, affectionate, sometimes erotic connections with other women.

Perhaps even more than her brother, however, the adolescent girl struggles with the rapprochement conflict. She is nourished by closeness and identity with mother, but this is the mother who so completely dominated her in the formative years. The girl very much wants and needs her own autonomy, but she is understandably reluctant to lose the emotional nourishment provided by identifying with mother. This conflict, mild or severe, is apt to accompany a woman throughout her life, in her relationships with both her mother and other women.

Jessica Benjamin points out that there is one more significant problem faced by the adolescent girl as she resolves her Oedipus complex. She was raised in a world in which masculinity, and particularly possession of the penis, is associated with sexual desire, with being the assertive actor in the sexual encounter.[13] Femininity, including the lack of a penis, is associated with passivity and submissiveness. She was taught that it is not feminine to *desire*. Rather she is to strive to *be desired*.

On the other hand, her history includes an important phase of identification with her father. It is very unlikely that her post-Oedipal identification with her mother has entirely eradicated that earlier stage. Thus, like the father with whom she identifies, she must unconsciously hunger for *agency*, not just sexual agency, but certainly including that. And once again she is confronted with the lack of a penis and all that that implies in this culture.

Thus, to the extent that she identifies with both parents, the girl is faced with the question: Can I have both agency and sexuality? Can I be allowed to be sexually active as well as passive? May I desire as well as be desired? Benjamin says: "The conflict between the identificatory love that enhances agency and the object love that encourages passivity is replayed over and over in woman's efforts to reconcile autonomous activity and heterosexual love."[14]

Freud observed that the path through the Oedipus complex was strewn with obstacles. Although he had no doubt it could be successfully traversed, he often seemed uncertain what it was that determined success or failure. His followers, studying the relationship between parents and children, observed that loving and sensitive guidance could go a long way toward maximizing the chances of a successful outcome. That guidance must include the parents' willingness to control the forces in themselves that tempt them to be excessively seductive or aggressive toward the adolescent.

The feminist psychoanalysts have added that, as gender equality progresses, there may be less and less need for boys to assert their identity by repudiating the feminine and ever more willingness to recognize and embrace the feminine in themselves. There will also be less and less need for girls to devalue their femininity. One of the most important marks of a successful Oedipal outcome is a loving and respectful relationship between the sexes, one in which we recognize our similarities as well as our differences. We might hope we are at the dawn of an age in which our culture will not only make that possible but support it.

We began this chapter by noting that Freud saw nothing mysterious about the problem of Hamlet's vacillation and paralysis. He thought that once it was understood that Shakespeare was writing from deep unconscious inspiration, the problem would clear up:

> The plot of the drama shows us . . . that Hamlet is far from being represented as a person incapable of taking any action. . . . What is it, then, that inhibits him in fulfilling the task set him by his father's ghost? The answer . . . is that it is the peculiar nature of the task. Hamlet is able to do anything—except take vengeance on the man who did away with his father and took that father's place with his mother, the man who shows him the repressed wishes of his own childhood realized. Thus the loathing which should drive him on to revenge is replaced in him by self-reproaches, by scruples of conscience, which remind him that he himself is literally no better than the sinner whom he is to punish. Here I have translated into conscious terms what was bound to remain unconscious in Hamlet's mind. . . . It can of course only be the poet's own mind which confronts us in Hamlet. . . . Hamlet was written immediately after the death of Shakespeare's father . . . , that is, under the immediate impact of his bereavement and, as we may well assume, while his childhood feelings about his father had been freshly revived. It is known, too, that Shakespeare's own son who died at an early age bore the name of Hamnet.[15]

Hamlet is understandably ambivalent toward his mother, treating her both angrily and tenderly. It is not hard to see why:

By betraying Hamlet's father, she has stirred Hamlet's deepest forbidden wishes. There is another woman in the play, the young Ophelia, with whom Hamlet has exchanged vows of love. Although we are told he has been very loving to her, when we see them together he is cold and aggressive. His behavior toward her is one of the fascinating puzzles of the play. One of the many possible explanations is that he is unconsciously repeating his ambivalence toward his mother. The way he treats Ophelia might also be seen as calculated to drive her away from him just as his mother went to another man. This would then be an instance of what Freud called the "repetition compulsion." To better understand how early experiences, including the Oedipus complex, influence our lives, it is useful to explore that process, which is the subject of Chapter 5.

5

THE REPETITION COMPULSION

The difference between rats and people is that when a rat gets shocked at one end of a maze, he never goes there again.
—B. F. Skinner, Harvard College Lecture, 1959

My client, Edward, had a habit of establishing a series of close friendships with couples near his age. In relationship after relationship, an erotic energy would appear between Edward and the woman of the couple and he would have to end his contact with them. Each time he felt terrible about it. He thought it co-incidence. Readers who have gotten this far will have suspected that Edward was in the grip of an Oedipal fixation. But they may well wonder, fixation or no, what unconscious forces would impel him repeatedly to put himself (and his unsuspecting friends) in the familiar, painful situation.

It is not just Edward who repeatedly manages to replay endless varieties of distressing situations and relationships. It seems to be common to the point of ubiquity. It is not difficult to find examples of the phenomenon we are about to explore.

> Marsha, the client of one of my students, had a father who was unusually charismatic, powerful, and successful. He was, not surprisingly, too busy to give much attention to his adoring daughter. Marsha, who was quite beautiful, seemed to have a fine radar for finding and attracting lovers who fit this profile. Whenever she did find a man who really loved her and was prepared to devote himself to her, she soon lost interest in him.

> Another client, Kevin, sought therapy because he found himself attracted to a succession of women who had had an unusually large number of lovers. After establishing the relationship, he was plagued by angry jealousy over each woman's previous lovers. It became clear to his therapist that he repeatedly provoked his lover into recounting stories of her past liaisons. His parents had been divorced when he was very young, and his mother had had a succession of live-in lovers. Kevin began therapy with no conscious awareness of the connection between his turbulent childhood and the paradox of seeking out women certain to stir his jealousy.

What we observe in these examples is what Freud called "the repetition compulsion." This phenomenon causes dismay when we see it in our friends and despair when we see it in ourselves. We have all breathed a sigh of relief when a friend finally exits from a destructive relationship, only to watch with disbelief as he or she begins another one, destructive in just the same way. Repeating the same unhappy situation over and over is a major cause of human misery and is one of the first things a therapist looks for when setting out to understand a client.

Freud put it like this:

> We have come across people all of whose human relationships have the same outcome: such as the benefactor who is abandoned in anger after a time by each of his *protégés,* however much they may otherwise differ from one another, and who thus seems doomed to taste all the bitterness of ingratitude; or the man whose friendships all end in betrayal by his friend; or the man who time after time in the course of his life raises someone else into a position of great private or public authority and then, after a certain interval, himself upsets that authority and replaces him by a new one; or, again, the lover each of whose love affairs passes through the same phases and reaches the same conclusion.[1]

Every semester I give my clinical graduate students a term-paper option of writing about the influence of the repetition compulsion on their current lives. I am no longer surprised by the number of students who choose this option. Many students describe the dismay with which they recognize that they choose a lover calculated to replay a particularly painful aspect of a parental relationship. The attribute might be suffocating invasiveness or cold non-responsiveness or frustrated love. It is as though the students unconsciously see themselves as directors repeatedly casting a drama about their childhood and searching for the perfect actors. Those students who are very sophisticated, or who have had a lot of therapy, add to the description of their skillful casting recognition of the ways in which they have unconsciously taught their partners to play their roles.

> Stephan's mother was a successful professor, apparently more interested in an intellectual relationship with her children than an emotional one. As a young child Stephan had found her fascinating, but he was often lonely and would gladly have traded in her intellectual stimulation for some elementary cuddling and loving. His current partner was a brilliant fellow student. Stephan reported that he had originally found her essentially lacking in the warmth he so craved, but he came to realize that he tended to withdraw in very subtle ways whenever warmth was offered. Thus it was offered less and less, and he found himself complaining that he had had the bad luck to pick a woman like his mother.

Often students write about their relationship with authority figures, occasionally with me. I found one student, Jennifer, more argumentative than the norm, and her arguments weren't always very friendly. At the end of the semester she wrote an intelligent and insightful paper describing her angry, rejecting father and her repeated attempts to provoke me into playing her father in the road company.

Like so much of human behavior, this seems paradoxical: Why go to such trouble to create a situation sure to cause one pain and frustration? When we examine the phenomenon closely, whether in ourselves, our friends, or our clients, it becomes clear that what is being repeatedly re-created is a very early, very painful situation.

At first glance, it looks as though the person were trying over and over to create a happy ending for that earlier situation. But as we have seen, it doesn't work that way. Should a replay turn out happily, the experience seems spoiled, and it's back to the drawing board to re-create the old unhappy situation once again. It is as though the very painfulness of the original situation was fixating, driving one repeatedly to behave as though he or she were unconsciously trying to understand what had happened and why it had happened. The situation with a happy ending would cease to be the *original* situation, which is defined by conflict, frustration, and guilt, and thus would lose its attraction.

Freud was fascinated by the repetition compulsion. He was puzzled by children playing the same game over and over. One such game he observed consisted of the child throwing a toy, saying, "Gone!," and then retrieving the toy. He felt certain this represented the mother going away. At first he thought the point was the retrieval, thus undoing mother's departure, but then he learned that the child could play the game for some time with apparent satisfaction, *omitting* the retrieval and just throwing a succession of toys out of sight beneath a table. Mother's departures were always painful, so why was the child playing them out over and over?

Freud's attention was then drawn to the operation of the repetition compulsion in the relationship between patient and analyst. He observed that patients often attempt to manipulate the analyst into repeating the parental relationship. Because the relationship being repeated was often very unpleasant—one with an angry or rejecting parent, for example—Freud thought it surprising that these people seemed to be needlessly courting what he called "unpleasure." How could he account for it?

Freud began to notice that it was not only in the psychoanalytic situation that the repetition compulsion appeared and not only with people he thought of as neurotic. It seemed to happen to a wide variety of people and in a wide variety of situations.

Freud ascribed great importance to the *pleasure principle*, as we saw in Chapter 2. Were it possible, he thought, we would lead our lives seeking out only pleasurable and satisfying experiences. The realities of the world and of our conscience make this impossible, so the pleasure principle is continually modified, often frustrated, by the *reality principle.* Under the sway of this principle we learn to avoid pleasures that will get us into trouble or to delay gratification to earn a greater gratification later. The repetition compulsion seemed to obey neither of these principles. It seemed to Freud, to his considerable surprise, that he had come across a force more powerful than the pleasure principle.

In 1920 Freud published *Beyond the Pleasure Principle,*[2] in which he tried to explain the repetition compulsion. He began by reporting his discovery that the event or the relationship being acted out represented a repressed memory. If his patient was trying to provoke him into hostility, Freud discovered that the painful *memory* of the hostile father was repressed. There was a conflict within the patient's mind. One of the primary laws of the unconscious is *that which is repressed seeks expression.* This expression would produce some of the pleasure frustrated by the repression. One of the primary laws of the ego is *that which is repressed is denied expression.* That is in fact what repression means. So the mind hits on the compromise of acting out the memory in a repetition. This gives pleasure to the repressed unconscious because it satisfies some of the desire for unrepressing, and it brings unpleasure to the repressing ego because it is too close to the original memory for comfort.

This formula was a nice try, but Freud knew it didn't work. Under the sway of the repetition compulsion, people repeatedly dream or act out replays of events or relationships that were never pleasurable in the first place; the pleasure principle has been soundly defeated. Besides, people often remember full well the original painful situation, so it doesn't seem even to have been repressed. Perhaps the need to make sense out of the pain in our lives, to understand what went wrong, is an important part of the motivation for the repetition compulsion.

Helping a client become free of the repetition compulsion is one of a therapist's greatest challenges. Often a client can be gradually liberated from such a compulsion by learning more and more of its manifestations, particularly how it manifests itself in the relationship with the therapist.

> After we had worked together for some time, a client, Caroline, once thought she saw a bottle of pills outlined in my jacket pocket and concluded they were antidepressants. She went on to say that she thought I sometimes had a melancholy air about me. If I did have a depression problem, she said, she must be a difficult client, because her bouts of sadness must make me feel worse.
>
> I believe I must always take seriously a client's perception of me, and I can believe that there is a subtle melancholy about me that a sensitive observer could pick up. But there were no pills in my pocket, and I had been feeling mostly quite cheerful in that period of my life. We talked about her concern for some time. I acknowledged that it was very likely she could see expressions in my face

of which I was not aware. I added that her interpretation of what she saw in my pocket was plausible, although there might be other explanations. She agreed. She said it comforted her to think I might be somewhat depressed because then I could understand her better. I considered this a breakthrough moment.

Caroline had a history of choosing difficult men, often men with drug problems, although she seldom used drugs herself. She was able to construct a different rationale for her attraction to each man; she believed she chose them in spite of the drug problem and the difficult relationship they offered her. During the first two years of therapy it gradually became clear not only that she chose them for their problems, but that she skillfully taught them to be difficult. She provoked fights and even encouraged their drug use.

The veils finally dropped off when, some months before our conversation about the imagined pill bottle, one of her lovers finally managed to join Narcotics Anonymous and stop using. Within weeks Caroline had lost interest in him. For a while it seemed to her that she had cooled to him because he had become boring and could only talk about his 12-Step meetings.

For a long time we had both believed that in the unconscious dynamics of her family system, Caroline had been appointed caretaker and therapist to her very unhappy older brother. In our work she came to realize that she had long concluded that in some unspecified way, perhaps by her very existence, she was the cause of her brother's distress, and that it was only fair that she should be his caretaker.

After the breakup of this most recent relationship, Caroline no longer doubted that she was repeatedly replaying her relationship with the brother. But the insight didn't help much; she continued to find herself attracted to the same kind of man.

Then came the incident with the imagined pill bottle and my melancholic expression. I asked her to explore her feelings further. She confessed that she sometimes worried that she made me sad and that when she thought I looked sad she tried to cheer me up by talking about happier subjects. She repeated that, in spite of that concern, she thought she was better off with a sad therapist. She thought a laughing-boy therapist would be hard to take.

I said I could really understand all of that. I asked her to tell me more about what made her think I was a sad or even depressed person. She said she often thought that her slow progress made me sad, especially her failure to stop joining up with such losers.

We talked about that for some weeks. I didn't need to point out that her relationship with me, like her relationship with her lovers, was another replay. One day she said, "So you're just another one of my brother-replays, aren't you?" When we parted, about a year later, she was dating a different kind of man.

You might be interested in knowing the next step Freud took as he worked at understanding this fascinating phenomenon. In *Beyond the Pleasure Principle,* he stated that he had come to believe the pleasure principle was, after all, not the most powerful force. He thought that he had discovered a regressive *instinct*. He now thought that there were two major forces operating in us, forces continually in mortal combat. The first such force consisted of the instincts of *Eros*, the life energy, which move toward bringing things together and moving life forward. The second major force consisted of the instincts of destruction, which move backward toward recovering the original state of the component parts of the universe. He thought that destruction included a "death instinct" continually struggling against Eros. Our aggressiveness and destructiveness all grow out of this second group of instincts. The repetition compulsion, he thought, is a manifestation of these regressive instincts, part of the death instinct, always struggling against Eros to move us back to an earlier state. Freud considered the repetition compulsion more powerful than the pleasure principle. He summarized these ideas in *Civilization and Its Discontents,* published 10 years after *Beyond the Pleasure Principle:*

> There still remained in me a kind of conviction for which I was not yet able to find reasons, that the instincts could not all be of the same kind. My next step was taken in "Beyond the Pleasure Principle" when the repetition compulsion and the conservative character of instinctual life first attracted my attention. Starting from speculations on the beginning of life and from biological parallels, I drew the conclusion that, besides the instinct to preserve living substance and to join it into ever larger units, there must exist another, contrary instinct seeking to dissolve those units and to bring them back to their primeval, inorganic state. That is to say, as well as Eros there was an instinct of death. The phenomenon of life could be explained from the concurrent or mutually opposing action of these two instincts. It was not easy, however, to demonstrate the activities of this supposed death instinct.[3]

Freud was fascinated with this dualistic view of the universe and clung to it until the end, in spite of his cheerful acknowledgment that it was speculation without evidence. Although the repetition compulsion is now a universally accepted and extraordinarily useful clinical fact, the riddle of its motivation remains essentially unsolved. In addition, although most psychodynamic theorists accept the presence of an instinctual aggressiveness, only the most orthodox Freudians find the theory of the death instinct clinically or theoretically useful. However it's hard to deny that there is a grand poetic power in Freud's view of the two colossal giants contending for our souls.

6

ANXIETY

What we clearly want is to find something that will tell us what anxiety really is.

—Sigmund Freud,
Inhibition, Symptom, and Anxiety

Everyone who attempts to understand problems in living, and everyone who attempts to alleviate such problems, has to deal with the issue of anxiety. We can provisionally define anxiety as a set of familiar, unpleasant physiological events—rapid heart rate and respiration, for example—that may or may not be accompanied by a cognitive explanation. That is, I may know why I'm anxious or I may not. In psychodynamic usage, anxiety has become synonymous with "fear." Freud once wrote that "precise language" would use *anxiety* when the person didn't know what he or she was anxious about and would use *fear* when he or she did. But that turned out to be more precise than he and most subsequent writers have found it convenient to be.

In Chapter 2, I observed that too little repression can get you into trouble by allowing unrestricted chaos to reign in your mind. We saw that too much repression can get you into trouble, also. Perhaps the same can be said about anxiety. As we examine Freud's theories of anxiety it will become clear (if it isn't already) that we couldn't get along without anxiety. Without some optimal amount of it we would walk blindly into serious danger. However, most of us are subject to a good deal more anxiety than is good for us, and anxiety resides somewhere in the causation chain of each of our problems.

Freud pondered the question of anxiety repeatedly. His very early papers were concerned with it, and he was still working on it at the end of his life. He began by positing that anxiety was caused by repression but, as we'll see, he soon found himself in a logical quandary. The history of his thinking about anxiety is one of the most interesting in the development of his theories.

The First Theory of Anxiety

At the beginning of his career, like a good nineteenth-century scientist, Freud thought in terms of physical models. One of these was a hydraulic model of energy under pressure, mentions of which are found in his earliest psychological writings, dating from 1897. He also thought in terms of physical principles, one of which was the "constancy principle," according to which energy systems tend to seek a constant state. When sexual desire is aroused and then blocked, it generates a quantity of energy under pressure. The tendency of an energy system to maintain a constant state causes the organism to seek a way to reduce this increased excitation. If this energy can't be discharged as sexual release, it seeks another way out. Freud thought the most likely releases were the physiological events of anxiety.[1] He was led to this theory by the observation of male patients who practiced *coitus interruptus*, sex without orgasm.

In his time, before convenient and effective birth control was widely available, *coitus interruptus* was fairly common. Freud believed that if a patient reported significant anxiety, there must be repressed sexual impulses behind it. The blocked energy may not represent anything as obvious as *coitus interruptus,* but Freud was certain there was some kind of sexual block. The theory was simple and neat and it fit well into the orderly biological system he was trying to construct. The only problem was that it contained a glaring logical inconsistency.

The Second Theory

Freud maintained his first theory of anxiety for many years. Then in 1926 he published *Inhibition, Symptom, and Anxiety,*[2] in which he pointed out the logical inconsistency, acknowledged that his previous theory was not good enough, and proposed a new theory of anxiety. This was one of several times in the development of psychoanalysis that Freud showed his readiness to change his mind when the data no longer fit the theory or when he saw a better way to conceptualize a phenomenon. As we enter a new century, Freud's second theory of anxiety is about 75 years old, but even so, many, perhaps most, psychodynamic psychologists who study the topic believe that it is still the best theory of anxiety that we have.

The logical inconsistency in Freud's initial thinking was this: If repression causes anxiety, what causes repression? If I have repressed some or all of my sexual impulses, why have I done that? It became clear to Freud that the only possible reason could be anxiety itself. If I were not afraid of *something* I would not have instituted this costly repression. One can imagine any number of things of which I might be afraid. I might be afraid of being physically hurt or punished in some way. I might be afraid of being tormented by guilt. I might be afraid that the impulses won't be satisfied and that I'll be painfully frustrated. If any of those fears were strong, a likely way of dealing with them would be to repress the dangerous impulse, in the hopes of eliminating the fear.

Freud said that it was no longer possible to say that repression causes anxiety because it seemed clear that the situation is the other way around: Anxiety causes repression. If we cannot say that anxiety is simply dammed-up energy leaking out of the system, how *shall* we understand it?

Freud abandoned his neat physical model and thought his way through to the psychological understanding that remains unsurpassed: Anxiety is the response to helplessness in the face of danger. If the danger has struck, the anxiety is automatic and immediate. If the danger is still in the offing, anxiety is the *anticipation* of helplessness in the face of danger. The overwhelming preponderance of anxiety falls into the category of anticipation.

If I see a lion about to attack me, I have a pretty good idea of what will happen in my body if and when he gets his claws into me. My heart rate will increase, my respiration will become rapid and shallow, and there will be manifestations of a sudden infusion of adrenaline. So as I watch him coming toward me, my body produces an attenuated version of those phenomena. It is saying to me, "You feel all this? This is nothing compared to what you'll feel if that lion actually reaches you." The perception of those bodily changes is what we experience as anxiety. Their function, Freud saw, was to serve as a *warning* of danger in the offing. The purpose of the warning is to signal us to take action against the impending danger.

We began this examination by noting that sexual anxiety might cause repression of the sexual impulses. How is this connection between sexual anxiety and repression illustrative of Freud's new theory? Imagine that I have been effectively taught, however subtly, that sex is somehow shameful. Imagine next that I am confronted with a sexual opportunity. I know only too well that if I follow the impulse I will feel painfully guilty. Freud's language for this is that I will be punished by my superego, that is, my conscience. Now the place of the attacking lion is taken by the threatening superego. As I anticipate the attack of the superego, the adrenaline flows, my heart pounds, and I am being warned to find a way to head off the danger or face still worse feelings. Repression of the sexual impulse is not the only possible solution, but it is a likely one. If I just leave the scene, I have to deal with the resulting frustration and possible regret. But if I succeed in repressing the impulse, I am spared both that frustration and the guilt caused by the superego attack. The anxiety has warned me of the danger from my superego. Repression will enable me to escape that danger and thus relieve the anxiety. Thus anxiety causes repression.

The repression may not be complete. I may find myself in the sexual situation with my performance and my enjoyment impaired by the partially effective repression triggered by my anxiety. This is a common compromise. It is as though I am unconsciously saying to myself, "I know I shouldn't be doing this, but if I don't do it well or if I don't enjoy it very much, perhaps I won't feel too guilty." Not doing it well is a distinct possibility in this situation: Often the effect of anxiety on the nervous system is to disrupt the performance and enjoyment of sex.

We could imagine other dangers associated with this sexual situation. We might be in a place where we could get caught in the act. We might be uncertain about how well we were protected against pregnancy or disease. Any of these could be the attacking lion and evoke the warning signal: anticipation of helplessness in the face of danger.

When I am scheduled to deliver a lecture for which I don't feel prepared, I feel all the bodily signs of anxiety. The danger is that I will make a fool of myself and be scorned by my students. I anticipate being helpless in the face of that danger, and my body is warning me to try to get out of the lecture. I used to fly small airplanes. If the weather were questionable I was apt to have an upset stomach the morning of the flight, even though I often did not realize consciously that I was afraid.

It is important to remember that Freud's theory describes not just anticipation of danger but also anticipation of *helplessness* in the face of that danger. If I feel confident of my ability to deal with the danger, I do not need to be warned and I do not experience anxiety.

I have said that the anticipation of danger produces certain bodily events. Freud understood this to occur because of how the body responds to the sudden increase of unpleasurable stimulation at the moment of birth. Since all carnivores and non-human primates experience similar bodily reactions to danger, this response to sudden unpleasurable stimulation seems neurologically hard-wired. In the womb, stimulation is modulated and controlled. At birth there is a sudden bewildering increase in stimulation that must be experienced as unpleasurable. The body of the infant responds with all the changes we have come to recognize as anxiety, including sudden massive changes in heart rate and respiration. Freud called this a "traumatic moment"; in fact, this is the original traumatic moment. Infants do not experience *anxiety* at this moment, however, because they cannot anticipate danger. But they can experience *helplessness;* there is nothing they can do about this new, unwelcome stimulation. This then becomes the prototype of helplessness in the face of danger.

Infants learn the great importance of mother's presence very early. If something unpleasurable occurs—hunger, pain, discomfort—infants are helpless to change it. Only mother, or her stand-in, can end the discomfort. It soon becomes apparent that it is important for mother to be present in case of emergency. Of course mother's presence is greatly desired for other reasons: She is the source of love and pleasure. But the *danger* of her absence is that no one will be there in case of trouble. This is the point (at about six or seven months) in infant development when *anticipation* is learned. This is a big step. When infants perceive mother's absence they now say to themselves something like, "I am not in any discomfort now, but I *may* be soon, and if I am, without mother here I will be helpless to correct it." Full-fledged anxiety—a warning signal of impending helplessness in the face of danger—is now possible. The infant experiences this anxiety and cries or calls, and, if lucky, has thus learned to head off the danger before it has actually occurred. From a survival point of view this anticipatory mechanism is extremely adaptive, but psychologically it is a slippery slope, because it will not be long before the child learns to fear, and thus inhibit, that which will cause mother to withdraw her love and her protection. The anxiety is triggered several long steps before the actual discomfort occurs.

I remember all too vividly my terror when I realized I had hurt or angered my mother. I was not raised in a violent house; I can't remember either parent ever striking me. I was seldom punished or had privileges taken away. Yet the slightest indication that I might be in trouble with one of my parents would fill me with fear. Freud traces this phenomenon directly from birth, the original traumatic experience. The next step is even more costly. The very *thought* of doing or saying something that would displease my parents soon came to trigger the anxiety. Freud thought that, throughout our lives, our cardinal fear is of losing a valued person or a valued object. Losing the *love* of a valued person is psychologically equivalent to losing the person. To Freud, the reaction to loss is pain, and the reaction to anticipation of loss is anxiety.

Freud divided anxiety into three categories: realistic, moral, and neurotic. Anxiety is a function of the ego, and the ego has three demanding forces with which it has to deal: the external world, the id, and the superego. Each of those produces its own anxiety. Realistic anxiety is fear of something in the external world (the attacking lion), and moral anxiety is fear of being punished by the superego. (If I do this contemplated thing, I am going to feel painfully guilty.) Neurotic anxiety is fear without a consciously recognized object. (I feel afraid and don't know why.) Neurotic anxiety stems from a buried impulse, one generated in the id. Once the hidden impulse is revealed, it turns out that the anxiety is either realistic or moral. The reason the impulse was frightening in the first place, and therefore repressed, is that acting on it will bring realistic danger or punishing guilt.

Freud gave the example of his child patient "Little Hans,"[3] who feared his powerful incestuous love for his mother. This was neurotic anxiety because its true cause was hidden from Hans; it was realistic anxiety because acting out this incestuous love could bring punishment in the external world. No reader who has gotten this far can doubt what Hans ultimately feared as the punishment for incestuous impulses. He feared being bitten by a horse, which Freud interpreted as fear of castration.

Freud thought that castration anxiety was the main cause of excessive repression and of neurosis in men. He pointed out, for example, how many men have an exaggerated fear of venereal disease, whatever precautions they may take. In women, he thought, excessive repression and neurosis are likely to be caused by fear of loss of love, stemming from the original fear of loss of mother's love. This is neurotic anxiety because the sexual impulse is partly or wholly repressed, and it is realistic anxiety because what is feared is a painful consequence in the external world.

Because neurotic anxiety is fear of an unidentified, unconscious danger, the therapeutic goal is to make the danger known so it can be dealt with. A good example is agoraphobia. Agoraphobics fear leaving the house, fear being in public, fear being in the street. They cannot tell why. They can only tell that those situations produce intense, often intolerable, sensations of anxiety. One discovered cause of agoraphobia is this chain: I am filled with unsatisfied sexual longings. Were I to act on them I would feel terrible guilt. If I go out in public I will encounter many people, and some of them will stir the temptation to act on my impulses. If the temptations are strong I will give in to them, and thus there is potential danger everywhere. I will lose the love and respect of the people I value. Perhaps I will contract a disease or, if I am a man, be hurt in some way. And above all my conscience will make me wish I had never been born. As I contemplate going outside I anticipate terrible dangers, and anxiety strikes, warning me to avoid the temptations of the streets. I cannot tell why the thought of going out is so terrifying; I can only tell of the terror.

The Involvement of Anxiety in Our Problems

I noted previously that anxiety lies somewhere in the causation chain of every problem; its importance cannot be overestimated. I once was evicted from an apartment I had lived in happily for some years. When I received the notice that the building was being sold and I would have to move, I experienced a severe panic attack. The attack subsided after a few days, but I remained extremely anxious. Although I soon learned there were other nice apartments in my neighborhood, that knowledge did nothing to reduce the anxiety. I had anticipated having to move for some time because the elderly landlord was failing and his wife had mentioned wanting to sell the building. The anxiety remained intense and subsided gradually only several months after I had moved into my new apartment. My therapist friends suggested that the anxiety was excessive. I tried to discover its roots, but each time I tried, the anxiety mounted and I quickly gave up the effort.

The external situation was real but trivial. Something unconscious had apparently become attached to it. A year after I moved I finally was able to search out the attached neurotic anxiety. When I was 13 my young father had a massive heart attack and died without warning. My grieving mother began to run, taking me with her. We immediately left our town, my friends, everything familiar. My mother went into seclusion, and for a time I lived in a strange place with relatives I hardly knew. When my mother recovered from her grief she returned to her premarital profession, acting. We lived together in a small apartment and I saw very little of her. I felt I had lost everything.

It is not difficult to imagine the neurotic anxiety that attached itself to the mild inconvenience of losing my apartment. The imminent death of my landlord, the imminent sale of the building, and the loss of my home stirred the old losses. But what was the neurotic anxiety? The reader, having read Chapter 4, will have a pretty good idea. I was 13, the time for sudden increased intensity of the Oedipus complex. We can assume that unconsciously I wanted my father out of the way and horribly got my wish. In the realm of primary process the wish is equivalent to the deed, so I was now guilty of patricide. The classic punishment for patricide is exile, Oedipus's fate. And exiled I was, thus confirming my guilt. To finish the drama, I soon found myself living with my young and beautiful mother in a one-bedroom apartment. Although I didn't see much of her, the fact remained that the Oedipal victory was complete.

When the childhood scenario was repeated, the ancient anxiety surfaced. This is what Freud called moral or superego anxiety. It is the fear that my conscience will punish me severely for the ultimate transgressions: patricide and incest. In addition, this new exile stirred the unconscious fears that the pain of the original exile would return.

What is the anxiety that causes Hamlet's paralysis? If his uncle deserves to die, then he, who is as guilty, deserves the same fate. Unconsciously he fears that if he kills his uncle he too will die, which indeed he does. He also carries unconscious superego anxiety, fearing that his conscience will punish him more severely if he kills a man who is no guiltier than he himself.

Anxiety is somewhere in the causation chain of every neurotic problem.

Janny, a lonely young woman client, knew she was hungry for contact and yet withdrew from potential friends or lovers whenever contact was offered. It took months for

her to discover her fear that contact would lead to intimacy and that intimacy carried some nameless danger.
The danger remained nameless until she connected her
fear of contact to a childhood event: When she was five
years old her beloved father, the only person in the family
she really trusted, had, without warning, abandoned the
family, never to be heard of again. It was a shattering
trauma. Slowly Janny learned that the unconscious fear of
abandonment struck whenever she anticipated intimacy.

Geoffrey, whom we met in the Chapter 4, is the Oedipal
victor who was left alone in an intense relationship with
his mother after the divorce of his parents. His problem
was sexual inhibition in his relations with his wife. Geoffrey unconsciously believed he had committed symbolic
incest by leaving his ejaculate visible on the sheet for his
mother to wash. By the logic of primary process, all sex, or
at least all sex with women, was sinful; thus the thought of
sex filled him with the unconscious fear of being punished
by his conscience. Also he believed that he belonged to his
mother and that he was committing infidelity by having
sex with anyone else. He was unconsciously afraid of his
mother's vengeance.

How Is Anxiety Relieved?

How is anxiety to be relieved, whether it is one of the presenting symptoms or a hidden cause? To the psychodynamic therapist the answer is clear. The anxiety is so strong and so disturbing for a concealed reason that must eventually be made visible.

Sometimes the passage of time will reduce it, as it did when I was evicted. Often it won't. Gregory had to learn a good deal about his relationship with his parents before his buried anxiety surfaced and then diminished, releasing him from his sex inhibition.

In addition to the psychodynamic method, there are two other major approaches to anxiety reduction. In "cognitive therapy" the client is helped to see that the frightening situation is actually less dangerous than it appears. The psychodynamic therapist understandably has questions about whether this reasonable approach reaches the unconscious roots of the problem. The cognitive therapist says that doesn't matter. The controversy remains unsettled.

"Systematic desensitization," developed in the 1950s by Joseph Wolpe,[4] a South African psychiatrist, is built on the model of classical (Pavlovian) conditioning. One of the observations made by psychologists who study learning theory is that an undesired response can be eliminated by teaching the subject an incompatible response. Wolpe reasoned that *relaxation* was incompatible with anxiety, and that if subjects were taught to relax in the presence of the feared stimulus, it would be impossible for them to be anxious. He further reasoned that the subjects were not going to have an easy time relaxing in the presence of something that frightened them, so it would be necessary to approach the fear gradually. Wolpe found that he could accomplish the anxiety reduction by merely having the relaxed subject *imagine* the frightening situation or imagine progressively more frightening aspects of the situation. Wolpe believed that every problem could be understood as a *phobia*, so he chose to develop his technique by treating phobias, that is, fear of an object or situation not justified by the client's own estimation of the danger. The client really does know that the odds against this airplane crashing are very great; nevertheless, as it begins its takeoff roll he is terrified.

Imagine a person with a fear of flying so severe that it limits her employment opportunities. Wolpe would have no interest in the client's past or unconscious. He would work with the client to develop a hierarchy of relevant frightening situations ranging from the mildest to the most severe. For example, the mildest might be hearing someone say the word "airplane." The most severe might be finding oneself in flight in the middle of a raging thunderstorm. Then Wolpe would teach his client a relaxation technique called "progressive relaxation," teaching her to relax while imagining the first item. When she could do that without anxiety they would move to the next item, and so on until she could imagine the most severe item without fear. Wolpe's research indicated that once a client had mastered the hierarchy of imagined situations, he or she could face the actual situation without crippling anxiety.

Wolpe's critics claimed that even if he could cure the phobia there was always the danger of remission or of symptom-substitution, because the underlying cause had not been dealt with. They added that the technique could not be applied to a problem like Gregory's because he had no conscious anxiety, just lack of arousal. From a scientific point of view, the jury is still out on the efficacy of Wolpe's technique.

One group of psychodynamic therapists who became interested in Wolpe's work pondered the following possibility: We believe the symptom is caused by an unconscious phenomenon, so there is necessarily an associative link between the symptom and that underlying cause. If the underlying cause is successfully dealt with in psychodynamic therapy, the symptom disappears. Is it not possible that the association chain could work in the other direction? That is, if the symptom is dealt with by a technique such as Wolpe's, might not the association chain weaken or even eliminate the underlying cause?

I once treated a man who had a panic attack each time he drove up the inclined portion of a bridge that lay on his commute. My client was a very successful man with graduate degrees. His father had been an angry and vindictive blue-collar worker. We worked for some months on my client's guilt about "rising above" his father and his fear of somehow having to pay for it. We also worked on the symbolic connection between rising above his father and "ascending" the bridge. In a few months his fear of the bridge disappeared. We continued for some years after that to work on other issues that troubled him. The phobia never returned. It is interesting to speculate on what would have happened had I chosen to treat the bridge phobia by Wolpe's technique and had I succeeded. Would the association chain have run backward and would we then have reduced his guilt and fear about surpassing his father? And would he have been protected from a return of the phobia?

All of this is just speculation. We should note that Freud would not have found this "backward" hypothesis very credible. Nevertheless, if a phobia is the client's main problem or if it is crippling, the most efficient psychological way of dealing with it appears to be Wolpe's systematic desensitization. Later the client might want to address other problems in a different kind of therapy. We also should note that important strides have been made recently in treating phobias with medication, particularly some of the antidepressants.

The efficacy of Wolpe's method implies that how a symptom was acquired does not necessarily dictate the best way to remove it. Freud could be absolutely correct about the genesis of anxiety, and it could simultaneously be true that some anxieties might be alleviated by techniques other than psychodynamic.

Understanding how we deal with anxiety was one of Freud's first concerns. It led him to the topic of Chapter 7, which we will consider next: the mechanisms of defense.

7

THE DEFENSE
MECHANISMS

The principal Freudian concept on which everything turns holds that
mental illness is a result of defense against anxiety.

—Peter Madison,
Freud's Concept of Repression and Defense

From almost the very beginning of our lives, we are presented with inevitable conflicts. There are peremptory impulses demanding satisfaction. Posed against them is the outside world, which threatens punishment for the attempt to satisfy many of those impulses. That is the first conflict, and in various guises it is lifelong. During childhood another force develops and must be dealt with: the superego, the conscience, which threatens the punishment of guilt. Psychoanalysis is the study of these conflicts and how they are dealt with.

In Freud's picture of our mental life, we have seen that impulses originate in the id, and the *ego* is that part of the personality charged with handling these conflicts among the id, the outside world, and the superego. The ego must try to keep us out of danger while attempting to get at least some of our impulses satisfied. It must try to keep our psychic pain to a minimum. Above all, the ego must keep us from being overwhelmed by all three varieties of anxiety: realistic, moral, and neurotic. This is not an easy assignment. The very anticipation of satisfying some of the impulses raises the specter of punishment and thus produces great anxiety. A conscious decision to forgo the impulse, however, may be severely frustrating.

To many of the ego's attempts to solve these dilemmas Freud gave the name *defense mechanisms.* Repeatedly he said that the defense mechanisms were the cornerstone of psychoanalytic theory. If we understood them we would understand how the mind works. Although he added that we would thereby also understand neurosis, it is important to note that neither Freud nor any of his followers believed that it was necessarily pathological to employ defense mechanisms. On the contrary, we all employ them; we couldn't get along without them. They become a problem only if they are employed by the ego excessively or inflexibly.

It is a commonplace observation in physical medicine that the body sometimes attempts to alleviate a disease or an injury with excessive enthusiasm and produces a condition worse than the disease or injury. Freud's statement that the defense mechanisms are the key to neurosis carries the same implication. In an attempt to protect themselves from anxiety, people sometimes institute excessive defensive measures that become persistent parts of their character and seriously burdensome.

Of the various mechanisms of defense, Freud first focused on *repression,* a mechanism we explored in Chapter 2, where we saw how excessive repression burdens our lives. Later Freud added other mechanisms, but he never got around to writing a systematic account of them. That task fell to his daughter, Anna Freud, who in 1936 published *The Ego and the Mechanisms of Defense,*[1] which is still one of the standard psychoanalytic books on the subject. From her father's writings she culled a list of defenses and then added a few; we will consider the most important here.

I would like to propose a definition of *defense mechanism* that departs from the classic definitions, a departure we'll examine later in the chapter. It has, I hope, the advantage of simplicity: *A defense mechanism is a manipulation of perception intended to protect the person from anxiety. The perception may be of internal events, such as one's feelings or impulses, or it may be of external events, such as the feelings of other people or the realities of the world.*

Repression

We can illustrate this definition by examining a mechanism with which we are already familiar, repression. Repression means excluding an impulse or a feeling from consciousness. Thus it is the manipulation of the perception of an internal event.

The erotic desire for a forbidden person is dangerous. If the person I desire is my parent or child or sibling, or perhaps (if I define myself as heterosexual) a person of my gender, being aware of that desire would put me in danger of painful guilt feelings. Were I to disclose the desire I would be in further danger, that of being shamed or punished. If I am aware of the impulse and manage to keep it entirely hidden, I must deal not only with the guilt but also with the frustration of a strong need that can never be satisfied. It seems clearly to my advantage *not* to be aware of the desire.

The same is true of aggressive impulses. It is hard for many people to be aware of angry feelings they harbor toward the people close to them. For some of us it hard to accept our angry feelings toward anyone. As with erotic feelings, it seems better not to be aware.

That option is available; it is the option of repression. We meet again our old friend, the watchman who guards the drawing room of consciousness. He examines this desire that is seeking admission to consciousness and decides to exclude it, to keep it in the entrance hall. If it has somehow managed to get into the drawing room, he escorts it out again. In the language of the theory of defense mechanisms, the ego has recognized this double demand of the id:

- that the desire be recognized consciously and
- that it be satisfied through action.

The ego well knows that if either of those demands is granted, the superego will attack with guilt. It also knows that there are likely to be negative responses from the outside world if the desire is revealed. So it represses the desire, that is, keeps it out of awareness, keeps it imprisoned in the unconscious, and in so doing protects itself from anxiety, from the anticipation of helplessness in the face of danger. We will see in Chapter 8 that, at least in the case of aggression, this is a Pyrrhic victory. The superego is not going to be mollified by the aggressive feelings having been made unconscious.* In the above example

---

*Freud was one of the most sophisticated neurologists of his time. Before he began his career as a therapist, he distinguished himself as a neurological scientist. He knew full well that there weren't three little people inside one's head arguing, threatening, and negotiating. The id, ego, and superego each represented a group of functions, aspects of the personality. He sometimes found it useful to speak of them as though they were separate entities, as I have in this paragraph.

a perception of an internal event (desire) has been blocked. I still desire the person or I still want to hurt the person, but that desire is now unconscious, out of sight, no longer perceived by me.

As we saw in Chapter 2, repression is indispensable. Incestuous wishes are a good example. Because few of us are planning to violate the taboos and take the consequences, it would be painful, frustrating, and guilt-provoking to be aware of those impulses. The same can be said for many of our erotic desires and many of our aggressive impulses. If we did not repress at all, we would be overwhelmed by the profusion of fantasies and impulses impinging on our consciousness.

As we also saw in Chapter 2, most of us repress more than is good for us. If I cannot be fully aware of my loving feelings, both tender and passionate; of my playfulness; of my assertiveness; and of my grief and sadness, my life is truncated and distorted. Although repression is indispensable when applied to appropriate impulses in appropriate doses, when overdone it is the cause of serious problems in living.

There is an important lesson about child rearing to be learned from this. Many of us were taught that not only were there good and bad *actions*, there were also good and bad *feelings*. It is a rare parent who encourages children to distinguish between feelings and behaviors by fully supporting their right to feel whatever they feel while teaching them that certain *behaviors* are proscribed. Encouraging that distinction, however, would go a long way toward protecting the child from excessive repression later in life.

Both Sigmund and Anna Freud thought that repression was the basic defense mechanism and the one that is most likely to cause serious neurotic difficulty. We will see that a couple of the others can be very destructive if carried to excess, but for the most part they are part of normal mental life. As we go along, we will consider the mechanisms labeled *denial, projection, reaction formation, identification with the aggressor, displacement,* and *turning against the self.*

Denial

Repression is the manipulation of the perception of an *internal* event. The mechanism of *denial* is the mental manipulation of an *external* event.

Denial means protecting myself from anxiety by failing to perceive or by misperceiving something in the world outside of my own thoughts or feelings. Once we are past childhood, denial presents a problem for the ego. One of the ego's assignments is reality testing. We survive by our ego's capacity to assess reality, and it is through that capacity that we maximize our gratifications. It is the ego that reminds us that as much as we might enjoy driving fast, the reality is that serious speeding is likely to get us arrested or killed. For the ego to use a defense mechanism in which it distorts reality, for example, that there is no danger in speeding, presents it with a problem. Nevertheless, even the most mature and flexible ego does at times manage to do just that.

A classic example of denial in our present world is the persistent unwillingness of large parts of the population to acknowledge known health risks, most flagrantly cigarette smoking. To smoke without a great deal of anxiety it is necessary to blot out awareness of the danger.

During the height of the nuclear standoff between the United States and the Soviet Union, all of the inhabitants of the planet were in continual danger of unthinkable catastrophe. I suspect that for everybody some degree of denial was necessary to live without crippling anxiety. Most people seemed to have managed a great deal of denial. Even anti-nuclear activists needed some to keep functioning.

Serious gamblers employ denial, to their considerable cost. The odds against winning one of the high-payoff lotteries are staggering. I have a friend who speaks of winning the lottery, and when someone says they didn't know he played it, he replies, "I don't, but I have as much chance of winning as people who do." That is very nearly true, yet there is no shortage of customers for lottery tickets. Committed slot machine players could not keep playing if they didn't deny the large odds against them. Even crap shooters, who face the least terrible odds in the casino, must deny what a small chance they have of coming out ahead in the long run.

Most of us use the defense of denial at least occasionally. Once at my job I very much wanted a certain assignment and for several weeks believed I was the front-runner for it. A friend, worried about me being crushed when the reality was revealed, took me aside and gently said that everyone but me saw that I didn't have a chance—my supervisor had been putting out clue after clue. I had not permitted myself to see those clues.

We sometimes employ denial in our relationships when, for instance, we are motivated not to see that our love is unrequited or, in the opposite case, when the relationship is so pleasant we refuse to see that we are getting in deeper than we intended.

Denial can be very dangerous, as in the smoking example. However, it can sometimes be adaptive. A friend of mine needed a biopsy, which, she was told, could result in either a harmless or a catastrophic diagnosis. The biopsy was scheduled for seven days after she received this news. She went about her business for that week quite cheerfully. I said to a wise psychologist friend of ours that I was worried about her denial, that I was afraid she would not be prepared for the catastrophe should it occur. My friend told me to leave her alone and be glad she had the ego strength to deny the danger when there was nothing she could do about it. I have never forgotten that advice. Incidentally, the story had a happy ending.

Projection

A defense mechanism in which we manipulate both an internal *and* an external perception is *projection*. Projection refers to protecting oneself from anxiety by repressing a feeling and misperceiving another person as having that feeling. I repress my anger and see you as being angry at me. I repress my lust and see you as lusting for me.

This form of projection, by the way, often accompanies homophobia. I repress my homosexual longings and believe that another man, perhaps one I identify as gay, is trying to seduce me. It seems likely that many of the political anti-gay accusations have their roots in projection. For example, it is often said that gay men shouldn't be allowed to teach school or be scoutmasters because they may promote a gay lifestyle or even seduce little boys. There is no evidence for this, so the theory of projection would imply that it may be the accuser who fears he is in danger of being seduced or of seducing. The reader will have no trouble understanding why so many heterosexual servicemen violently object to having openly gay men in their unit.

Freud believed that homophobic projection could explain many cases of paranoia.

> One of my clients, Jay, was a doctoral student trying for a long time to complete his dissertation. Month after month he became progressively more incensed at the professors on his dissertation committee, claiming that they managed never to run out of new obstacles to put in his path. Finally he concluded that they didn't want him to get his degree and that they were conspiring to defeat him. Throughout this period I became increasingly convinced that he was sabotaging the dissertation, and that he was unconsciously determined not to finish it. His father had been a blue-collar worker who had made real sacrifices so that his son could pursue his education and who had died just as Jay began graduate school. Jay spoke often of his love for his father, his gratitude for having been encouraged to obtain an education, and his sadness that his father had not lived to see him complete it. Gradually it became clear that he also felt very guilty about surpassing his father. The guilt was multi-determined because his father's death left him in sole possession of his mother. The whole complex of emotions was so frightening to Jay that his solution was to project onto the professors his sense of being unworthy and the wish that he fail.

We all employ mild versions of projection a good deal of the time and never notice it unless it affects a relationship enough to call attention to itself. It is not uncommon to project on one's partner the fantasy of infidelity and them blame him or her.

When I was in college, a friend of mine who was very close to his roommate became unshakably convinced that his fiancée was planning to have an affair with his roommate during a time my friend was to be out of town. In an intense confrontation, his very cool and sophisticated fiancée said to him, "Someone wants to sleep with Ted, all right, and it isn't me." My friend was thoroughly shaken. Later he said to me that until that moment he had firmly believed that his heterosexuality was unalloyed. When he heard in a psychology course the theory that everyone was unconsciously bisexual, he thought, "Except me."

This situation turned out to be a mild (and very instructive) problem. Projection carried to extremes can become a very serious problem, worsening until it is full-blown paranoia.

Reaction Formation

Reaction formation is a defense mechanism in which we protect ourselves from anxiety by manipulating an internal perception. It means misperceiving a feeling as its opposite. Often it means turning love into aggression or aggression into love.

One of the most fascinating and heartbreaking episodes in the life of Beethoven involved his nephew Karl and his sister-in-law Johanna, Karl's mother. Beethoven conceived an unreasoning hatred of Johanna and a firm conviction that he must rescue Karl from her. Beethoven's most psychologically sophisticated biographer, Maynard Solomon,[2] makes a compelling case that Beethoven's obsessive hatred of Johanna represented a passionate unconscious attraction to her.

An extremely important form of reaction formation is mis-perceiving a *wish* as a *fear*. It is a common way of protecting oneself from guilt over a wish.

> My client Marian was concerned about the physical safety of her 10-year-old son. She kept him on a tight leash, restricting his freedom considerably more than did the mothers of his friends. She expressed continual anxiety that something terrible would happen to him. Before the birth of this, her only child, she reported having been a cheerful and carefree person. A prolonged post-partum depression followed her son's birth. It was to be the first of a series of painfully severe depressions. Marian spoke often about how very much she loved this boy and how much she worried about his safety. It was many months before she could tolerate exploring the possibility that perhaps she felt anger as well. It was many months after that before she could allow me to say, "We both know that he intended you no harm. Nevertheless it seems to me inevitable that once in a while you could wish some punishment on him for damaging you so."

We saw the classic example of a wish underlying a fear in Chapter 3 when we looked at anally fixated people whose fear of dirt and messiness masks the wish to be allowed the freedom they were denied as a child. In moderate doses this is relatively harmless. However, carried far enough, this form of reaction formation can produce a distressing neurosis.

Psychodynamic therapists have learned that when confronted with a client's fear that the therapist finds puzzling, they should wonder, at least silently, what wish that fear might mask.

The opposite form of reaction formation is *counter-phobia*, protecting oneself from having to confront a fear by misperceiving it as a desire.

I am fascinated by cutlery stores. There is a chain of them in New York with large picture windows displaying an endless collection of shiny knives, razors, and scissors. I can spend a lot of time in front of one of those windows, although I certainly don't need yet another Swiss army knife. A reader who has gotten this far will recognize a counter-phobic response to a serious case of castration anxiety.

Identification with the Aggressor

One of the most important parts of Anna Freud's book is her chapter on identification with the aggressor.[3] Although Sigmund Freud had described the phenomenon in several contexts, he never isolated and named it.

It is very anxiety provoking to be confronted with someone more powerful than you who has aggressive intentions toward you or who you fear may have such intentions. It may also be anxiety provoking to have aggressive intentions toward that powerful person, because of the fear of retaliation. Identification with the aggressor is a defense designed to protect one against the anxiety stemming from conflict with a powerful person or from being at the mercy of such a person.

In Chapter 4 we saw that identification with the aggressor plays a major role in the resolution of the Oedipus complex, in the formation of the adolescent's identity, and in the formation of the superego.

The psychoanalyst Nancy McWilliams[4] has pointed out that Anna Freud's discussion of this phenomenon would have been clearer had she called it "introjection of the aggressor," because that is clearly what she meant. Identification usually implies a less automatic and unconscious defense than introjection. Children *identify* with their parents, mentors, or peers in pretty obvious ways: dress, attitude, and mannerisms. They also *introject* aspects of them, as in the resolution of the Oedipus complex. Introjection implies unconsciously assuming that a given attribute or collection of attributes of the other person resides in me. However, we will stick with Anna Freud's vocabulary because it has an apparently permanent place in the language.

Identification with the aggressor enables me to increase *my* perceived power by introjecting some aspect of the dangerous person. I may introject one or more of his or her personal characteristics; I may introject the aggressiveness; I may introject both. In the classic Oedipal resolution I become like my same-sex parent in that I define myself as heterosexual and set out to find my own mate. It is probable that I become like that parent in a lot of other ways as well. I construct some important part of my identity through this introjection.

In this defense I may also use *projection*. I project my aggressive intentions onto the other person to protect myself against superego anxiety, that is, to protect myself from guilt. Thus I'm not aware of feeling aggressive toward my father; I'm only aware of *fearing* him. Because I have introjected his power, the fear is manageable. Children who play at being omnipotent superheroes are employing an everyday, adaptive version of this defense. They are, of course, identifying with a fearfully powerful person, often a parent.

In his book on the Nazi concentration camps,[5] the psychoanalyst Bruno Bettlelheim, himself a holocaust survivor, gives a heartbreaking example of this defense. Jewish prisoners identified themselves with their Nazi guards. They imitated a guard's walk and mannerisms and seized a discarded bit of a guard's uniform as a prized possession.

Displacement and Turning Against the Self

Anna Freud tells of a woman patient whose attempts to deal with anxiety illustrate two defense mechanisms that we have not yet considered:

> When this patient was a child she suffered from acute envy and jealousy of the favored treatment she believed her mother accorded her brothers. This eventually turned into a fierce hostility toward her mother, and she became overtly angry and disobedient. But her love for mother was equally strong, putting her in severe conflict. She feared that her anger would cost her the love she so desperately needed from her mother. As she entered the latency period, her anxiety and conflict became more and more acute. Her first attempt to master this anxiety was to employ the mechanism of *displacement*. In order to solve the problem of her ambivalence she displaced the hatred onto a series of women. There was always in her life a second important woman whom she hated violently. This produced less guilt than hatred of her mother, but it was not guilt-free. So displacement was not an adequate solution.
>
> Her ego now resorted to a second mechanism [which Sigmund Freud called *turning against the self*]. It turned inward the hatred which hitherto had related exclusively to other people. She tortured herself with self-accusations and feelings of inferiority. Through ado-

lescence and into adulthood she did everything she could to put herself at a disadvantage and injure her interests, always surrendering her own wishes to the demands made on her by others.[6]

Like the other mechanisms, displacement and turning against the self are familiar in everyday life and are relatively harmless as long as they are mild and short-lived. Displacement is such a common defense that it has acquired a common nickname: "Kick the dog." After my boss treats me badly it's clear I can't *express* my anger to him. What is more subtle is that I may not even permit myself to *feel* it fully because it will make my work life unpleasant and because it may stir unconscious guilt about feeling anger toward a parent. At such times my near and dear give me a wide berth; they are safer targets.

> My client, Victoria, learned as a child that expressed anger had dire consequences, often days of receiving the silent treatment. She grew up all but incapable of even *experiencing* anger, let alone expressing it. Her response to any interpersonal difficulty was to feel quite depressed. It took her a long time to be able to see the depression as anger turned against herself, the only safe place to direct it.

At the beginning of this chapter I proposed a definition of *defense mechanism*: A defense mechanism is a manipulation of perception intended to protect the person from anxiety. The perception may be of internal events, such as my feelings or impulses, or it may be of external events, such as the feelings of other people or the realities of the world. I stated that it differed from the classic definitions. That difference raises a fascinating issue.

Anna Freud wrote that "defensive processes, such as displacement . . . or turning against the self, affect the instinctual process itself; repression and projection merely prevent it being perceived."[7] She meant that the child in the example quoted above from her book really did stop hating her mother and started hating first the other women, then herself. The change was not merely perceptual. My proposed definition implies that the hatred of mother is still present unconsciously and is merely repressed, that is, not perceived.

It is not unusual to work with a client who has displaced his or her erotic Oedipal longing onto another person and then betrays unmistakable evidence that the original longing continues to exist unconsciously.

When Freud devised his second theory of anxiety in 1926, it had an impact on his theory of defenses. The reader will recall that the 1926 theory described anxiety as a signal, warning of impending helplessness in the face of danger. The defenses are meant to protect one from that sense of helplessness. Adult anxiety, Freud thought, was exacerbated by serving as a reminder of the very early traumatic situations when the newborn, infant, or child was flooded with traumatic intensities of stimulation. Thus an important function of the defense mechanisms is to head off that traumatic stimulation.

One of the three kinds of anxiety with which the defenses have to contend is moral anxiety, fear of the superego. That raises one of the major issues for psychodynamic psychology: the problem of guilt, which is the subject of Chapter 8. Let's explore that now.

8

GUILT

The cost of advanced civilization is the sense of guilt.
—Sigmund Freud, *Civilization and Its Discontents*

This is the startling premise of Freud's major study of "civilization's" development: We have sacrificed our happiness for advanced civilization, and the mechanism of our unhappiness is an increasing sense of guilt, often guilt over unconscious impulses. In this chapter we will explore Freud's understanding of how and why our happiness has been lost and how that understanding relates to his theory of the superego.

A client of mine was maneuvered into agreeing to help a colleague with a difficult job. It was a commitment she really didn't want to make. After thinking it over she mustered the courage to back out of the commitment. The colleague to whom the commitment had been made angrily accused her of reneging on a promise. My client's first response was rage. She hadn't wanted to make the commitment in the first place, and she thought she had been shamelessly manipulated. The rage lasted about 30 minutes and then was replaced by a painful feeling of guilt. She told herself she had no right to let her colleague down, no matter what her desires.

This scenario, or one like it, is distressingly familiar to many, although probably not all, of us. We might think of this as *noisy* guilt, guilt that announces itself with such fanfare that it is impossible to mistake. Those of us subject to this kind of guilt, who often feel terrible about what we've done, said, or even thought, know this as one of life's truly heavy burdens. Those who have a particularly serious case of this kind of guilt don't even require that the other person become angry or remonstrate. Just asserting oneself is enough to trigger the guilt. This is familiar territory; for many years there have been books and workshops devoted to helping those suffering from noisy guilt.

Fancied sins of omission can trigger this guilt as readily as sins of commission. I have a client who for years experienced a background guilt that appeared whenever he was not distracted or occupied. He believed there were always things he should have done or should do. Sometimes he could name the undone tasks; often they were nameless.

Then there is "quiet" guilt. Quiet guilt doesn't announce itself *as* guilt the way noisy guilt does. Quietly guilty people punish themselves in ways puzzling to the untrained observer, ways that cause psychodynamic therapists to infer that unconsciously they are trying to reduce a bit of quiet guilt by bringing punishment or failure on themselves.

Some years ago a major presidential contender was publicly accused of flagrant adultery. He denied the charge indignantly, saying, "If you don't believe me, follow me."

That night he kept an all-night date with his lover. The reporters called his bluff, and the next morning his presidential hopes permanently vanished.

Students "forget" the date of a crucial exam for which they are well prepared.

An employee insults her boss shortly after she learns she is being considered for a desired promotion.

A man finally persuades a passionately desired woman to go to bed with him and then, to his dismay, finds himself impotent.

In addition to "noisy" or conscious guilt and "quiet" guilt, which doesn't *feel* like guilt but merely arranges punishment that unconsciously seems deserved, there is "silent" guilt. People afflicted with this don't feel guilty. They don't incur inexplicable punishment. They simply feel like bad people a good deal of the time or they feel some vague unhappiness and discontent. In the final analysis this is the form of guilt that is most common, most serious, and, because it is constant, most destructive.

In Freud's view, human beings, unhampered, will selfishly pursue their interests, their satisfactions, and their pleasures. If anyone or anything interferes they become angry, and, if they believe themselves strong enough, they will unhesitatingly remove the obstacle. When many people live in close proximity*

---

*To Freud any group larger than a nuclear family living in close proximity and interdependent in some way constitutes a "civilization." This would seem to include all cultures almost from the very beginning. A great *many* people living in close proximity and interdependent constitute an "advanced civilization."

this tendency, if uninhibited, would lead to chaos. There is no evidence that Freud knew *The Leviathan* by Thomas Hobbes (1651), but the point of view described here is identical with the one proposed in that work. Like Hobbes, Freud thought that for civilizations, particularly advanced civilizations, to exist, it is necessary for there to be a mechanism for suppressing this uninhibited, self-centered aggression. An external authority is a partial solution, but authorities can't be everywhere. An *internal* mechanism is needed, an internal representative of authority that can be on the job at all times and in all places. Freud's view was that this necessity caused such an internal authority to evolve in the human species and become increasingly severe.

To a modern biologist this must seem a dubious understanding of evolution. That need not concern us; it is enough to note that whatever might have been true of early homo sapiens, modern humans certainly do contain this internal authority, and Freud has given us a powerful description of its characteristics. We have seen in Chapter 2 that this is the part of the personality to which Freud gave the name *superego*. In Freud's view it develops in the following manner.

If young children are left ungoverned they will pursue their pleasures and their satisfactions freely. In the beginning it is necessary to regulate them physically to keep them from interfering with the satisfactions of others. However, soon the mere presence of parental authority becomes enough to inhibit the child. To Freud this is an important step in the development of the superego. *Why* is the mere presence of the authority enough to stop children from pursuing their interests? Children quickly learn to anticipate punishment, even a punishment as mild as remonstrance. If I pour the custard onto the rug, my mother will speak harshly to me and that will feel bad. But why will it feel bad? I will have had the fun of pouring the custard, and mother's subsequent words won't actually hurt me. It will feel bad because I am rapidly learning how *very* important it is that mother *love* me. I am totally dependent on her; I cannot survive without her. None of my needs will be met if she abandons me. That includes my physical needs and my emotional needs. I *need* her to love me. Once learned, the danger of losing mother's love echoes throughout our lives.

> One of my clients began therapy assuring me that her relationship with her mother was satisfactory—nothing particularly significant in it. I soon learned that she repeatedly has the following experience: For some good reason, she will find it necessary to break a date with a close woman friend. This is followed by a severe anxiety attack. When I inquire, she explains the anxiety by saying that she is afraid that her breaking the date has made her friend angry. She has been through this sequence countless times; at their next meeting the friend is always thoroughly reassuring. That reassurance doesn't prevent the next anxiety attack. After months of work, she began to recover memories of seeing a distant look on her mother's face that convinced her that she had somehow driven her mother away. Her unconscious fear of losing her mother's love translates into marked insecurity with her women friends.

Next comes the step Freud thought most important, indeed essential. There are not nearly enough police or parents to be everywhere. What keeps us from selfishly imposing our pleasure-seeking on anyone weak enough? Of course there are many people who do just that, and so we have problems of crime and of the strong exploiting the weak. But if everyone did it, we would have the chaos that would be the end of civilization. Most people don't do it. Most people don't do it even when the authority is not physically present. Why not?

There are two reasons. The first is now obvious from our story so far: We are afraid someone will find out and punish us. The punishment may be the dangerous loss of love or it may be actual physical punishment. My client is afraid her friend will be angry. I am afraid of getting speeding tickets.

But what if there is no chance of anyone finding out? What if the authority is *really* absent? Why then would I deny myself my natural satisfaction-seeking impulse? Freud teaches that we could not get along with each other even as well as we presently do if the only protection we had from the natural selfishness and aggressiveness of our neighbors was their fear of external authority. Some more omnipresent and threatening authority is necessary.

We opened this chapter by invoking the name of conscience, or in Freud's vocabulary, superego. The final step in our story is taking the authority inside our heads so it is always with us and its judgment always a danger. Conscience is that authority taken inside. If the first reason for denying ourselves satisfaction is fear of punishment from outside, the second possible reason, even in the absence of authority, is that the absent authority isn't really absent at all. He or she or they are very much present—inside our heads. Thus there is still danger of punishment: torment by the superego. In our mental life it is to that torment that we assign the name "guilt." When we resist a forbidden pleasure, we resist it out of fear of that torment, and when we give into it we might have to pay for it with the suffering the superego can wreak on us. Freud used the word "remorse" to describe the punishment by the superego for a forbidden action.

It's not difficult to imagine what that authority is that lodges itself inside our heads. Originally and most powerfully it is of course the parents. One of Freud's most valuable insights was into the phenomenon of *identification.* It tells us a great deal about how we take aspects of others into ourselves to form our personality. Our parents are the first and the most powerful objects of identification. We saw in an Chapter 4 that an important mechanism of the resolution of the Oedipus complex is identification with my feared rival, the parent of the same sex. An important aspect of that identification is the parent's function as law-giver and enforcer. Both parents say, "Thou shall not" about many things, and in the case of the Oedipus complex it is my rival who says, "Thou shall not covet my partner." Through this identification I take into myself these prohibitions, including the prohibition against incest. As I take them in, they become major aspects of my superego.

There is an important difference between external authority as judge and superego as judge, and this is the difference with which we have to deal as we strive toward allowing more joy and fulfillment into our civilized life. The difference is this: External authority can know only our actions and thus can punish only our actions. The superego, being inside our head, knows not only our actions but our wishes, our fantasies, and our intentions. It is not mollified by our assurances that this fantasy was *only* fantasy and there was no thought of carrying it out. It lives by the rule of primary process, in which the wish is equivalent to the deed. Thus it will punish us for an intention as well as for an action. On some occasions the punishment may possibly be as severe as if we had carried out the intention.

Soon we will explore the idea of mere thoughts making us feel guilty—how that can occur is not immediately obvious. But if we can demonstrate that Freud is right that thoughts can make us guilty, then it becomes clear that our happiness and peace of mind are in a precarious position. Imagine living surrounded by very strict police who punish slight infractions of a rigid code. That wouldn't be much fun, but presumably one could learn to be very careful and thus stay out of trouble. Next imagine that this strict code includes your spoken thoughts. This we know is galling, but careful people can still avoid drawing unwelcome attention to themselves. But now imagine that the police have invented a mind X ray that reads *thoughts,* and that forbidden thoughts are severely punished. You might start planning to emigrate.

In the absence of a forbidden action, are we likely to feel guilty over a mere thought or intention? Some people some of the time, some people a *lot* of the time, feel consciously guilty, indeed *very* guilty, about their thoughts. The most obvious examples are devoutly religious people who believe that certain thoughts are sinful, in fact, that many of their thoughts are sinful. There are familiar instances of religious people subjecting themselves to the most severe deprivations and austerities in an attempt to rid themselves of these sinful thoughts. There are many stories of saints trying to beat or starve sinful thoughts out of their bodies, including the following one about St. Francis:

> For, if, as happens, a temptation of the flesh at times assailed
> him, he would hurl himself into a ditch full of ice, when it was

winter, and remain in it until every vestige of anything carnal had departed. And indeed [his followers] most fervently followed his example of such great mortification.[1]

Many people who don't aspire to sainthood have an occasional thought or wish about which they feel consciously guilty. It is not uncommon for a person who feels burdened by a loved invalid relative to suddenly discover in himself the wish that the relative would die and release him. Nor is it uncommon for a father to suddenly discover that his daughter has become a woman and recognize a burst of lust toward her. Either of these discoveries might well be followed by an attack of conscious guilt.

However, most of us, most of the time, do not experience conscious guilt over a mere thought or wish. If I pass up the longed-for chocolate cake or the forbidden person of the desired sex, if I resist the impulse to say something really nasty to my antagonist, I may well feel some wistful regret, but it's unlikely that, consciously, I will feel guilty about the desire.

Although I may not feel consciously guilty about these desires, forbidden wishes are not overlooked by the superego. The functions of the superego are largely unconscious, and its great power depends on this. Were my superego entirely conscious I would be able to accept or reject its injunctions according to my enlightened adult standards. If it warned me against an action that was forbidden when I was a child, my adult ego could simply reject the injunction, recognizing that it is no longer valid or relevant. But we know that the unconscious doesn't play by those rules. In the realm of primary process there is no past or future. Ancient injunctions are as current today and as rigidly enforced as they were when I was a child. Because this is the realm of primary process, the wish is as sinful as the act and must be punished. Psychoanalytic theory is a theory of internal conflict, of a mind divided against itself. There are few more vivid examples than the punitive aggression of the superego toward the ego.

We began this chapter by noting that in addition to the noisy guilt and the quiet guilt we all know so well there is also silent guilt. We can now see what that is and how it comes about. When my superego punishes me for a forbidden wish, it all happens in the veiled realm of the unconscious and takes the form of unconscious guilt. Because it is unconscious I don't recognize it as guilt, and I don't know for what I am being punished. I only know that I feel bad; I feel a vague unhappiness and discontent.

There is a terrible irony in this: The more virtuous I am, the more likely I am to experience this silent guilt. Freud pointed out that the autobiographies of the saints are filled with lamentations of sinfulness. Freud explained this irony by saying that just as each satisfied impulse reduces the frustrated longing for that pleasure, each denied pleasure increases that longing. The more that longing increases, the more punitive the superego becomes. Freud thought that repressed aggressive impulses were particularly likely to give rise to this silent guilt. There is a clear implication in Freud's later work, particularly *Civilization and Its Discontents,* that, although a "civilized" individual might imagine how sexual satisfaction could be compatible with civilized life, there is no way to imagine that one's aggressive impulses could be satisfied without destroying the community. Thus those impulses are likely to be the most severely repressed and, by Freud's reasoning, produce the most severe silent guilt.

When we were children, each denied impulse mollified the authority and protected us from guilt. I restrained myself from hitting my younger sister and was rewarded with my mother's approval and the absence of guilt. However, once the authority is in my head with access to my wishes, things are reversed. Each denied impulse now *increases* my guilt.

Freud described this situation in this manner:

> Renunciation now no longer has a completely liberating effect; virtuous continence is no longer rewarded with the assurance of love. A threatened external unhappiness—loss of love and punishment on the part of the external authority—has been exchanged for a permanent internal unhappiness, for the tension of the sense of guilt.[2]

We human beings have a strong need to live in groups, to live close to each other. But this need conflicts with our innate aggressiveness and our desire to selfishly satisfy ourselves. To Freud, the solution seemed to be the development of conscience. Had conscience restricted itself to restraining our outward aggression, and had it done that a good deal more successfully than it has, it would have been a satisfactory solution. But it goes farther than that: It attacks us for our *thoughts*, thoughts over which we have no control. Freud believed that this was not true of everyone. He believed that there was wide variation in the frequency and severity of guilt attacks. Not everyone, he said, experiences the frequent bouts of unhappiness and discontent that are the expression of unconscious guilt. But he thought most of us did, and the superego's attack on us for the thoughts over which we have no control led him to say that the price we pay to be able to live in proximity and interdependence with each other is a loss of happiness through a sense of guilt.

I would like to illustrate the damaging power of unconscious guilt by describing two of my clients. Although one of them was consciously aware of feeling guilty and the other was not, in both of them the destructive guilt was deeply buried.

Jerry is the client I mentioned previously in this chapter who much of the time felt a nagging guilt about things he should have done that he had not. Whenever he accomplished a task that had been plaguing him, it was immediately replaced by the next one. He thought of it as his magic "to-do" list that added two items every time he removed one. In our high-speed world almost everyone has the sense that the to-do list is ever-growing. Some people accept this with wry amusement, some find it merely annoying, but there seem to be many, like Jerry, who experience real guilt over it.

Jerry has a childhood memory that often occurs to him. He had a great deal of admiration for his father and also a considerable amount of fear. He wanted his father to think well of him and usually doubted that he did. When he was about 12 years old he said to his father early one evening, "I've finished my homework. Can I go down to the corner?" His father's reply burned a permanent place in his brain: "You're not getting all 'A's." The implication was unmistakable: There is always more to do. It's unlikely that this single incident was the sole cause of his non-stop guilt as an adult, but it symbolizes an attitude that he had internalized from countless experiences. If he wanted his father's admiration he had to work ceaselessly for it. And even then, since there was no end to the necessary tasks, obtaining that approval was hopeless. When he began working with me his father was long dead. Now it was his superego telling him he was never finished and punishing him for the (often nameless) undone tasks. Also, underneath that identification with his father was his unconscious anger at his father for having saddled him with unobtainable goals. To the harassment for the undone tasks, the superego added punishment for this unconscious anger.

Kimberly came to me when she was in her early twenties. She seemed to have every asset; she was bright and charming and beautiful. Her presenting problem was that she had not dated since high school and not very much then. Although she did not mention it, she also seemed to me to be mildly depressed. She did her best to avoid men and, when she could not, refused their invitations. She had no idea why. Neither did I for several months. Then one day a female coworker said to her very warmly, "Kimberly, you really are beautiful." Kimberly's reaction was remarkable. She blushed furiously, left the room hurriedly, and then had a severe panic attack. By our next session she had become calm enough to begin to explore the meaning of the incident. Over the next months the story unfolded. She had a young and very attractive mother who, it appears, was not prepared to be so utterly outclassed by her daughter. When Kimberly reached adolescence and it began to become clear just how beautiful she was, her mother apparently saw herself as the dethroned beauty queen and became seriously depressed. Her mother's competitive feelings were never discussed, and

Kimberly had no conscious awareness that she was the cause of her mother's depression. She had only the faintest intimation of just how beautiful she herself was. Very gradually, in her therapy, she pieced the story together from fragments of memory.

Apparently Kimberly's father was devoted to his wife and altogether appropriate in his relationship with Kimberly. Nevertheless, however well Kimberly managed to conceal it from herself, her mother saw her as the Oedipal victor. Unconsciously Kimberly came to hate her beauty and blame herself for her mother's anguish. It was unthinkable to her that she could capitalize on her appearance by attracting men. Much of the time she managed to deny to herself that there was anything unusual about the way she looked. It also became clear that she could not permit herself to feel truly happy. Because she believed she was to blame for her mother's unhappiness, her guilt denied her the right to any happiness for herself. The reader, having by now been immersed in the theory of the Oedipus complex, will have detected another, deeper, source of Kimberly's guilt. Her mother had sent the message, "I surrender; you have conquered me." Thus Kimberly's unconscious distress over her triumph was compounded by the conviction that she had willed it.

For Jerry and Kimberly to be thus plagued, it was necessary that the causes of the guilt be hidden from them, that those causes be repressed. The goal of therapy was to create the conditions under which each of them could gradually recover the relevant memories and make the relevant connections.

In Chapter 11 we will explore the power of *transference* in the therapeutic relationship, that is, the way early parental relationships are superimposed on the relationship with the therapist.

Jerry's therapy provided a dramatic instance of the therapeutic value of transference. After some months of therapy Jerry was able to tell me he had become convinced I disapproved of him, that I didn't believe he took his work seriously and I suspected he was being overpaid. For some time I just empathized with how distressing that must be for him. Eventually I suggested that he had good reason to suspect that an older man in an authority position might disapprove of him: He had a historical precedent. Because he had learned not to question authority, the disapproval must be justified. Jerry saw that although that logic could readily be sold to a child, it was hardly airtight. Soon after that he was able to begin considering the possibility that his father had had some problems of his own, and that there was no commandment that said, "Thou shall be productively occupied every waking moment." By the time we parted, his guilt had eased considerably.

Kimberly and I worked a long time before the critical transference phenomenon turned up. We went through long months of exploring her fear of men and her discomfort over the idea of dating. We also saw the depression I had only suspected appear full-blown. Then I began to notice that in spite of the depression, she began showing up for her appointments more made up and dressed up than I had seen before. I am not usually reticent about sharing such observations, but I found myself reluctant to bring it up and was puzzled by my reluctance. I learned the source of the reluctance when I finally brought myself to mention her clothes and makeup. In the unconscious communication that takes place between client and therapist, I must have learned that this was an extraordinarily embarrassing topic for her. In the next session the clothes and makeup were back to their previous state, and she begged me not to mention them again. I said I could see how terribly distressed she was, and I dropped the subject. After some weeks I asked her if it was possible her depression had deepened because of feelings she was having about the therapy and about me. She said she thought it was possible. She was finding the therapy increasingly uncomfortable and was considering stopping. I returned to the forbidden topic of her clothes and makeup, saying that it would make a lot of sense to me if she had become aware of hoping that I found her attractive. I said that I knew it seemed to her that such a hope was shamefully self-centered, but that it seemed perfectly natural to me.

Over the years I have developed considerable respect for the wisdom of the unconscious. When I attend to its messages it will often steer the therapy far better than I could. I believe that Kimberly's self-exploration had brought her to the point where, just below consciousness, she was beginning to understand the dynamics of her inhibitions and was sending me messages, however ambivalently, that she was ready to enter the forbidden realm. As an adolescent she had indeed gone through a period when she had hoped her father would find her attractive, that he would find her very attractive, that he would find her more attractive than mother. Father never showed any signs of wavering in his devotion to mother, but Kimberly came to believe that her selfish wish had caused mother's distress. She had been punishing herself ever since. I am convinced that her wise unconscious produced the wish that I would be attracted to her as a way of leading us into her relationship with her father. It seemed to me a case of her awakened desire for growth finally overcoming her guilt.

It was many more months before Kimberly could tolerate any but the most tangential discussion of these themes, but eventually the depression subsided and she began dating.

I began this chapter by noting that Freud identified guilt as the high price we pay for civilization. For many of us the attempt to reduce guilt, avoid it, or expiate it is a major motivator as well as a significant energy drain. *Civilization and Its Discontents* is a gloomy book. More than 20 years earlier Freud had written a far more optimistic treatise[3] expressing the hope that a progressively enlightened civilization could relax the harsh sanctions on various forms of self-expression, indeed on the pursuit of pleasure. By 1930, when he wrote *Civilization and Its Discontents,* he had lost much of that optimism. It's impossible to identify all the reasons for that change, but certainly the horrors of World War I were a major factor.

However, Freud had not lost *all* of his optimism. Not everyone was subject to attacks of guilt over private thoughts; there was wide variation in the frequency and severity of such attacks. Not everyone, he said, experiences the frequent bouts of unhappiness and discontent that are the expression of unconscious guilt.

The therapy Freud originated has come a long way since 1930. So has our understanding of child-rearing and the possibilities of creating a more benign society. We have seen in this chapter that much of the suffering of guilt can be relieved in therapy, and perhaps in the new millennium many parents will learn how to raise their children so that fewer and fewer of them carry a heavy burden of guilt.

9

DREAMS

Ladies and Gentlemen,—It was discovered one day that the pathological symptoms of certain neurotic patients have a sense. On this discovery the psychoanalytic method of treatment was founded. It happened in the course of this treatment that patients, instead of bringing forward their symptoms, brought forward dreams. A suspicion then arose that dreams too had a sense.

—Sigmund Freud, *Introductory Lectures*

Freud considered *The Interpretation of Dreams,*[1] published in 1900, his most important book. Indeed, it contains remarkable riches. It introduces the Oedipus complex, the distinction between primary and secondary process, the infantile origins of adult functioning, and much more. Yet Freud was so proud of this book not because it described these momentous discoveries but rather because, as its title makes clear, it announced to the world that, in his opinion, he had done what no person before him had been able to do: break the code of dreams. He knew this was an important achievement in its own right; in addition, he was convinced that it unlocked the key to understanding and treating neurosis. If a therapist did not interpret dreams, Freud had come to believe, he or she was not doing psychoanalysis.

Freud's first major insight into the nature of dreams was that, like daydreams, night dreams represent a wish. Daydreams express a wish that the person can acknowledge, at least privately. As a child I daydreamed about being a star baseball player on my city's major league team. I had no shame about it at all. My friends had similar dreams, and we shared them freely. Now I occasionally daydream about being able to spend an entire Sunday morning in a coffee shop with the New York Times—guilt free. I'm not ashamed of that one, either. Taking his cue from daydreams, Freud reasoned that night dreams might also be the expression of wishes. He discovered that children's dreams are often as naked an expression of wishes as are daydreams. Freud reported that one of his daughters, after a day of illness-induced fasting, dreamed of strawberries, omelet, and pudding.

Freud observed that in some adult dreams as well, the wish is so transparent that little or no analysis is needed to understand it. He reported that if he ate salty food at dinner, that night he was invariably awakened by thirst. Before waking he always dreamed that he was enjoying the most delicious, satisfying drink imaginable. Then he woke up and had to have a real drink. His being thirsty caused the wish to drink, and the dream represented the fulfillment of that wish.[2]

However, such transparency is rare. In dreams that most richly illuminate unconscious forces the wish is concealed; that was Freud's next important insight. He taught that the only way the wish can be discovered is by encouraging the dreamer to associate freely to the dream elements.

It is not difficult to see why Freud thought dream interpretation was so important. He believed that all dreams were constructed in the same way that neurotic symptoms were formed. Because he believed that removing a neurotic symptom depended on learning its unconscious meaning, interpreting a dream would be a step toward cure, because the meaning of the dream would reveal part of the meaning of the symptom. His elegant system has turned out to be too simple, but it still contains remarkable insights into our dream world.

Freud's Model

- *Neurosis:* Neurosis is caused by the repression of unacceptable sexual wishes. The repression has not been sufficiently complete to protect the person from unconscious guilt, thus the distress of the neurosis. The buried wishes are under pressure seeking expression, and they find that expression in neurotic symptoms. In an attempt to at least avoid the conscious guilt, the incompletely repressed wish is disguised so that it can bypass the censor that repressed it in the first place. Thus the symptom must be decoded to reveal its unconscious meaning.

- *Dreams:* Buried wishes find their way into dreams. Detecting a relaxation of the censor during sleep, the repressed wish attempts to take advantage of this opportunity to achieve expression. However, although relaxed the censor is not off duty. Some ego-function on nighttime guard duty recognizes that the undisguised wish would cause sufficient anxiety to waken the sleeper. So although it lacks its daytime power to repress the wish, it manages to disguise it and thus (usually) protect the sleeper's rest.

- Unacceptable, disguised wishes cause the neurotic problem and must be decoded. Unacceptable, disguised wishes that generate the dream can be decoded, thus unmasking one of the symptom-generating wishes.

We can see why Freud called dream interpretation the royal road to the unconscious and why he thought it was the indispensable key to psychoanalyzing neurosis.

Freud's model no longer fully describes the psychoanalytic theory of neurosis. Although repressed sexual wishes probably do play an important role in many problems of living, they are no longer seen as the only cause. As we have seen in previous chapters, a wide variety of unconscious wishes and fears can generate problems.

The Origin of the Dream

Freud found that dreams were a response to something the dreamer had experienced the previous day. Some chain of associations to that event (which may have been a thought or an actual event) led to a wish that had to be repressed, being unacceptable to the dreamer. As the censor relaxes during sleep, the wish seeks expression.

What the Censor Does

Freud called the remembered events of the dream its manifest content. The concealed wish he called the latent content. The censor converts the latent content into the manifest dream by distorting it. The main processes by which distortion is effected are condensation and displacement. The following case study is an illustration.

> A client of mine dreamed he was watching a movie being filmed. A pair of horses was being driven to the edge of a cliff with the intention of forcing them to fall to their deaths. Although the dreamer knew it was a movie and that the animals were completely safe, he had to turn away as they approached the cliff edge.
>
> His first association was to associate "whores" to horses. He then remembered a phone conversation with an old friend that had taken place the day of the dream. Many years before, he and that friend had earned their college tuition by hiring out as "dance companions" on a cruise ship. In the previous day's phone conversation the friend, reminiscing, had said, "We were just a couple of whores, weren't we?"
>
> They had both enjoyed the cruises and being sought-after men. My client recalled that on one cruise his friend had broken the cardinal rule and slept with a very attractive passenger. My client was very jealous, of his friend's rebellious courage and, most of all, of his enviable sexual experience.

His associations to the apparent, but not real, danger to the horses:

> It looks like the horses are abused and murdered victims. I'm sure the truth is they are pampered movie stars. I imagine the same thing is true of some high-class prostitutes, too. Everybody pities them and thinks of them as abused and helpless drug addicts. But I imagine some of

them have a wonderful life—lazy luxury, immersed in the world of sex.

I said it sounded as though he might be envious.

You know, I think that's true. I really am fed up with this bourgeois life I've designed for myself. I think I have a secret hunger for the underworld, for the "demimonde." I would love to be a whore. I would love to be a high-end whore like we were on the ship, except I would sleep with the passengers and be paid a lot. I would be paid a lot, but the most important reward would be the endless sex-without-responsibility. I am sick to death of my bourgeois responsibilities.

This is as far as we will follow this dream here. Like most dreams, this one contains a whole nexus of meanings, only a few of which we unearthed. Some psychoanalysts have said, at least partly seriously, that if you fully understood any one dream of a given patient, you would understand the entire analysis. I confess I am happy when my client and I work out one useful meaning for a dream.

In this dream the generating day-residue is the client's phone conversation with his friend and the latter's remark about them being whores. The latent content is the client's wish to be free of his responsibilities and to find a sexual paradise. "Whores" are displaced onto horses. An entire saga is condensed into the single image of him watching the filming of a brief movie scene.

It is far from obvious that most dreams represent wishes. Yet after interpreting countless dreams of his own and his patients, Freud was convinced that wish fulfillment characterizes all dreams. His critics challenged him by citing anxiety dreams and punishment dreams. The latter he could easily deal with, once he had added the superego to his system: Punishment dreams represent the fulfillment of a wish of the superego, one of whose most important tasks is punishing its host for wishes it considers unacceptable. Anxiety dreams gave Freud more trouble, and 30 years after the original publication of *The Interpretation of Dreams* he was still revising the book, wrestling with that problem. Now, with 100 years of hindsight, it is probably safe to say that although the wish-fulfillment theory is very helpful in understanding a dream, no single formula can do justice to the richness of our dream life. We will consider this further below.

In the days before I began writing this chapter I had been futilely scouring Freud's books and papers to find another suitably illustrative dream. The night before I began writing, I had a dream that I remembered uncharacteristically well. I almost never remember my dreams, so this was an unusual gift from my unconscious.

I am a member of a football team, in the locker room, about to take the field to begin the game. The team is composed of both men and women. We are all in regular street clothes. I recognize the women as former students of mine. I realize there must be more than 11 of us about to take the field. Even though it's not my responsibility—I am just a player on the team—I make it my duty to count players, while thinking, "Isn't there an assistant coach who is supposed to be responsible for this?" I start counting heads out loud and Mimi Rollins starts saying random numbers in a loud voice to distract me. I become furious and say, "That's very rude and besides it's not funny; it's just stupid." I say the last word with such emphasis that it strikes me as unnecessarily aggressive, given the triviality of Mimi's fault.

I awakened pleased and grateful for having been given this needed dream. I then set out to explore my associations.

I saw Mimi last week. She looked good. Counting the players is the way I count chairs before the students arrive for my class. Sometimes while unstacking the chairs and counting them, I say to myself that I really don't think this is the instructor's job, but I always do it anyway. I regret stopping my college football career. I now see stopping it as a mistake. I find the girls on the team attractive. What I said to Mimi is an unpleasant paraphrase of a favorite movie line: the Debra Winger character in *Shadowlands* decking a sexist fool with, "Are you trying to be rude or are you just stupid?" Mimi Rollins leads me to Mimi in the opera *La Boheme*. I think of my friends Bill and Sarah and the days when Bill adored the opera and opera records and they worshipped Pavarotti. In those days Bill and Sarah were very much my father and mother. They fed me and took care of me and clearly loved me a great deal. I loved staying at their house. After Sarah's death all that changed. My mother-figure was gone, and the circumstances of my life had changed so that I got to Bill and Sarah's city less often.

My interpretation:

I will settle for just one of the possible interpretations. As I ponder the dream and the associations, it seems to me the dream reveals a powerful unconscious longing to be taken care of, to be a dependent child. In my conscious waking life I am compulsively responsible and caretaking. The dream says I have a lot of anger about assuming that role. My father died when I was 13 and my mother withdrew into her grief, leaving me pretty much on my own for some years. When she did show up it was more as seductress than caretaker. I have long known that was psychologically costly, but my knowledge is merely intellectual. The intensity of the longing with which those losses left me, and the anger at having been abandoned, caught me by surprise as I interpreted the dream.

Dream Symbolism

From the beginning of his work with dreams, Freud was interested in dream symbols. For example, a king and queen in a dream represent the dreamer's parents, the prince or princess the dreamer. Freud became convinced that symbols, particularly sexual symbols, could be reliably interpreted and could throw light on the latent content of the dream. He realized the risk: symbol-interpretation put the interpreter in danger of imposing his or her fantasies on the dreamer; interpretations generated by the dreamer's free associations, on the other hand, seemed more trustworthy. Nonetheless Freud came to believe that, in spite of the risks, the most powerful way to interpret a dream was to combine the dreamer's free associations with the interpreter's knowledge of universal symbols.

In the first edition of *The Interpretation of Dreams* there was very little mention of symbolism. In each of the next two editions Freud gave the subject more attention. By the fourth edition there was an entire section devoted to the topic, which Freud had studied at length and about which he cared a good deal. His writing on dream symbolism seems to reveal a certain ambivalence. On the one hand, given his concern that psychoanalysis not be seen as flaky or occult, he was extremely reluctant to seem to be writing a new "dream-book." In Freud's day, as in ours, there were books that told the reader how to interpret a dream so as to obtain specific advice from it. The advice might be about love or business or practically anything; it included specific predictions about how a given venture would turn out. This was done by translating certain symbols. For example, in one such book dreaming of a letter meant trouble ahead. Funeral meant betrothal. If the dream contained both a letter and a funeral, the dreamer was instructed to put them together and anticipate trouble for someone's betrothal. In certain American subcultures such books are still common. Often they give advice about gambling decisions, although, like the nineteenth-century books, they still also give life advice. At least since Freud's day, most educated people and certainly all scientists have looked on such books as superstitious nonsense.

Freud was anxious to avoid any hint that he was writing another such book. On the other hand, the more he studied symbols in dreams, in folklore, in popular linguistic idioms, and in jokes, the more he became convinced that he was justified in ascribing meaning, particularly sexual meaning, to dream symbols. Elongated objects stood for the male organ; hollow, receptive objects for the female sexual and reproductive system; and climbing stairs or ladders for sexual intercourse.

Freud remarked that it is not difficult to see how climbing can represent copulation. He pointed out that in climbing we come to the top in a series of rhythmic movements, there is increasing breathlessness, and then with a few quick jumps we once more reach the bottom. The rhythmic pattern of copulation is reproduced in going upstairs.[3]

Dream interpretation began to include careful attention to the dreamer's associations, as well as a cautious interpretation of dream symbols by the analyst. "Cautious" meant that even though the symbols seemed to have universal meaning, it was still important to pay careful attention to the context in which the symbol appeared.

In the days after I wrote the first part of this chapter, I searched Freud's examples of dream symbolism to find a useful illustration of dream symbols, not finding one I felt satisfied with. Then my unconscious obliged once more with a relevant dream, this one loosely tied to characters in a well-known opera, Mozart's "The Magic Flute." In the opera, Sarastro is the archetypal good father. He puts Tamino, the hero, and Pamina, the heroine, through some dangerous initiation trials, but only because he wants them to replace him as leaders of his community. He allows Tamino to play his protective magic flute as he and Pamina go through the trials. Sarastro's major aria concerns his commitment to forgiveness and to the rejection of vengeance.

> The dream: I am walking in a field near a river when a man approaches and asks me to help him fix an intricate device made of various kinds of metal. I start to take it apart, taking pins out, hoping I will be able to remember where they go when it's time to reassemble it. I get most of it apart and work

on a small cast-iron section whose disassembly is a puzzle—one part must be moved in a special way to free another part. While I am working on it I realize we are doing this for Sarastro and I see near us his flag in the shape of a conical hat. I wait and listen, hoping to hear Sarastro's big aria come out of the flag. Then I realize that when I was a boy Sarastro took me walking through the fields near here. I manage to finish taking the remaining section apart, all the pieces fall on the ground, and I am awakened.

Associations: The magic flute is not just any phallic symbol, it is a symbol of a powerful phallus. Manipulating the puzzle is masturbation. Sarastro made the magic flute from a tree in the forest during, I believe, a thunderstorm. Sarastro, the ultimate caretaker father, is a loving philosophical leader who doesn't believe in vengeance. He willingly gives his flute (= penis) to Tamino. He protects Pamina from her dark mother. One of the real terrors in the moments following my father's death when I was a boy was that now there was nothing between me and my mother. I tried to lock myself in a room to avoid her hysteria. Consciously to avoid her hysteria and unconsciously, I am certain, to avoid the sudden Oedipal proximity. I often saw my mother as dark and dangerous. I like being asked to help. I always do. That's part of needing to be responsible. I'm sure it is guilt-reduction and maybe shame-reduction. I remember once driving along feeling upset about something or other, when a car stopped me and the driver asked for directions, which I was able to give. My mood brightened dramatically.

Like all dreams, there are many meanings to this one. Following is one interpretation.

I long for a father who will support, not disapprove of, my sexuality: childhood masturbation and adult heterosexuality. I long for one who will enthusiastically make me the heir to his phallic power, and one who will forgive, truly forgive, my Oedipal rivalry, hostility, and eventual (bitter) triumph. I long for one who will protect me from my tempting, dangerous mother. Maybe if I'm a helpful person it will make him more willing to forgive me and support me.

It is clear why Freud saw dream interpretation as a crucially important tool in the treatment of neurosis. Neurosis is caused by unconscious conflict. How is that conflict to be discovered and revealed to the patient? Although the patient's free associations about matters other than dreams would hopefully reveal much about the conflict, there seemed to Freud only one certain way, "the royal road": dream interpretation.

The Current State of Dream Interpretation

A century after the publication of *The Interpretation of Dreams*, the relationship between psychoanalysis and dream interpretation has changed vastly. Many psychoanalysts no longer consider dream interpretation a central part of their work. The psychoanalyst Paul Lippman writes that, except for the followers of C. G. Jung, who continue to emphasize dream-work, the analysts' love affair with dreams seems to be over.[4] He ascribes this to theoretical shifts, including, surprisingly enough, a gradual de-emphasis on revealing the unconscious. This is associated with the move toward a kind of relational therapy in which the relationship between therapist and client is examined, not so much to reveal the unconscious as to replace such revelation.

Lippman also ascribes another cause to this move away from dreams. He says that analysts have always been ambivalent about working with dreams. He points out that Freud taught us to interpret dreams. That implied an obligation to outwit the dream-censorship and solve the dream-puzzle. Sometimes, often in fact, the censor wins, forcing the analyst to retire in confusion or perhaps find a way to blame the dreamer. That can end by making the analyst feel inadequate and embarrassed. Small wonder, Lippman says, that analysts were relieved to have a good reason to free themselves from the burden of dream interpretation.

Lippman adds an interesting speculation. We live at a time when our culture is turning away from the natural world toward the virtual one. It seems the external screens are becoming more interesting to us than the internal ones. Dreams are perhaps the most internal of all, so psychodynamic therapists turning away from dreams may be an expression of the spreading ambit of the electronic world.

I believe that for many depth psychotherapists, the move away from dream interpretation does not imply a lessening of interest in the client's unconscious process. Although some relational therapists are moving away from an emphasis on revealing the client's unconscious, that is by no means true of all of them. Merton Gill,[5] the godfather of relational therapy, and Heinz Kohut,[6] the founder of the school of self-psychology, were both firmly committed to the importance of bringing to the surface the ancient, buried roots of the client's problems in living. Many of their contemporary descendants still hold to that commitment.

Believing as he did that dreams were the royal road to the unconscious, Freud would undoubtedly be saddened to see dream interpretation vanishing from mainstream clinical practice. But it turns out that dreams are by no means the only such road and maybe are not even the most reliable. There is a great deal to be learned about clients' unconscious processes by attending to the details of their history, the subtle patterns of their lives, and the way they build the relationship with the therapist.

Nevertheless, psychodynamic therapists have probably given up too much in turning away from dreams. Pondering them adds richness to our lives and to our clinical work. It is regrettable, as Lippman says, that analysts developed the misconception that each dream conceals a meaning that must be quickly arrived at if the analyst is to seem competent. That takes both dreamer and listener away from the dream itself much too quickly. There is much profit in leisurely pondering the manifest images. In the first dream described above, I might have spent more time on the football game and my regret at having given up my college football career. I might have explored my feelings about working around numbers of attractive women. Certainly my attraction to the line from *Shadowlands* seems very promising. The interpretation I arrived at is undoubtedly revealing and useful, but it may only begin to mine the dream's riches.

It is unlikely that dream interpretation will ever again occupy a central place in depth psychotherapy, except that practiced by the Jungians. To the Jungians the royal road leads to more than just the patient's individual unconscious. Believing as they do that we all share a universal "collective unconscious," they see dream symbols as the necessary clues to the aspects of that collective unconscious now influencing the patient.[7]

In spite of many non-Jungian therapists turning away from dream interpretation, it seems likely there will always be psychodynamic therapists of every school still fascinated by dreams who will find working with them productive. Perhaps dreams are not the royal road to the unconscious, or at least not the only such road. Nevertheless they contain significant riches. When a dream (our own or a client's) is explored, less as a challenging code and more as a powerfully personal poem, explored leisurely with no particular concern for its meaning, it can be illuminating and enriching.

10

GRIEF AND MOURNING

What, man! Ne'er pull your hat upon your brows.
Give sorrow words. The grief that does not speak
Whispers the o'erfraught heart and bids it break.
—Shakespeare's *Macbeth*

In 1917 Freud published a short paper entitled "Mourning and Melancholia,"[1] in which he began the psychoanalytic exploration of loss, bereavement, and mourning, an exploration that turned out to be one of the more important contributions psychoanalytic thought has made to our understanding of human suffering. Since publication of that first paper, psychodynamic therapists have carried that exploration forward, so that grief and mourning are now among the best understood and most thoroughly explored issues that concern therapists, indeed that concern us all.

The aspects of "Mourning and Melancholia" that concern us here are these: When people are very important to us we invest a great deal of psychic energy (libido) in them and in our relationships with them. That energy is invested not only in the people themselves but also in all the important memories and associations connected with those relationships. The more important the relationship, the greater the amount of our psychic energy invested. That becomes clear when we think of a parent's investment in a young child. If the child dies or is lost in some other way, all of that invested energy is now homeless, producing acute pain in the bereaved person, followed by an intense, futile longing for the lost child. Whenever any important person is lost, the bereaved typically experience a major loss of interest in the world and in other people. It is difficult for them to conceive of conducting a relationship or forming a new one. They are grief-stricken; the intensity of that grief is a function of the importance of the lost relationship.

Now the mourning begins. Freud observed that the process of mourning was the painful, often laborious retrieving of the psychic energy from each important memory and association connected with the lost person. As the mourning progresses, the pain diminishes; when it is complete the person once more has his or her energy available to connect with the world, to invest in other relationships.

Freud's words on this subject are worth quoting:

In what, now, does the work which mourning performs consist? I do not think there is anything far-fetched in presenting it in the following way. Reality-testing has shown that the loved object no longer exists, and it proceeds to demand that all libido shall be withdrawn from its attachments to that object. This demand arouses understandable opposition—it is a matter of general observation that people never willingly abandon a libidinal position, not even, indeed, when a substitute is already beckoning to them. This opposition, can be so intense that turning away from reality takes place and a clinging to the object through [hallucinating it]. Normally, respect for reality gains the day. Nevertheless its orders cannot be obeyed at once. They are carried out bit by bit at great expense of time and psychic energy, and in the meantime the existence of the lost object is psychically prolonged. Each single one of the memories and expectations in which the libido is bound to the object is brought up and [intensely] cathected, and detachment of the libido is accomplished in respect of it. . . . When the work of mourning is completed the ego becomes free and uninhibited again.[2]

We will see that soon after writing this paper, Freud made an important change in this theory.

In Chapter 7 we discussed the "introjection of the lost object." Freud introduced the concept of the "introjection of the lost object" in this paper. He thought that it was sometimes an aspect of the melancholia, or depression, that follows a painful loss. By introjection of the lost object he meant that the melancholic person acts as though unconsciously he or she believes that the lost person is actually now a part of him or her. This is most likely to happen if the relationship was a highly ambivalent one. In that case the person becomes painfully self-critical. Freud observed that the content of the reproaches could best be understood as actually referring to the lost person, not the bereaved. His memorable phrase was, "the shadow of the lost object falls across the ego." He saw this introjection as a way of staving off the loss and also of clinging to a last opportunity to express the angry side of the ambivalence.

> My client, Scott, was a young father whose wife was tragically killed. As he mourned her in my consulting room, he began to experience intense guilt. At first he couldn't discover what he felt guilty about; he only knew he felt guilty. Then the

content of the guilt dawned on him: He felt terribly guilty for abandoning his six-year-old son. He accused himself of allowing himself to become so immersed in his grief that he had emotionally withdrawn from his son.

After some time it began to seem to me that in his account of their life together there was no evidence that he was indeed giving his son inadequate love and attention. I cautiously inquired whether he might be angry at his wife for abandoning them both. At first he rejected this suggestion heatedly, reminding me that there was no way his wife could be blamed for the accident in which she had died. Feelings that accompany grief are not always reasonable, I suggested, and it would be entirely understandable that among all the feelings accompanying the loss of his beloved wife might well be anger at her for leaving them. When he was finally able to explore that possibility, his guilt disappeared and he was able to begin mourning in earnest.

In "Mourning and Melancholia" Freud implied that introjection of the lost object occurred only in pathological grief reactions. He also said that successful mourning necessitated the withdrawal of loving energy from the images of the deceased, because if one clung to an internal image of the lost person, that clinging would interfere with the bereaved person's freedom to invest fully in new relationships. It does seem that one possible result of an unsuccessful mourning process is just such enthrallment. However, five years after he wrote "Mourning and Melancholia," Freud changed his mind. In *The Ego and the Id*[3] he wrote that introjection of the lost object, far from being pathological, may well be universal. It may be the only way one can give up a lost object and may be one of the important processes by which character is formed. Harvard psychologist John Baker[4] surveyed the contemporary psychoanalytic literature on bereavement and, as Freud suggested in this later paper, found widespread agreement that *successful* mourning often leaves the bereaved person with some benign internal image of the lost person. This may take the form of comforting memories or fantasies. Baker says that "benign" means that the bereaved have no sense of being haunted or possessed, and that they can call up the images when it suits them. Successful mourning means in part that those enduring images of the lost person do not limit the libido the bereaved has available for forming new relationships.

One of the many things Scott provided for me was the kind of clinical experience that must have led Freud to revise his theory of internalization of the lost object. Freud had originally thought that it was only in unusually ambivalent relationships that the shadow of the lost object might fall across the ego. All relationships are ambivalent to some degree, and it's likely that Scott's relationship with his wife was no exception. But I got to know him well, and I don't believe that, as relationships go, his was unusually ambivalent, meaning that there was an unusual amount of anger buried beneath Scott's considerable love for his wife. My clients, including Scott, have taught me that not only is introjection of the lost object very common, but unconscious anger at the lost person can masquerade as guilt in any lost relationship. Most psychodynamic therapists, including Freud's followers, now believe that the introjection of the lost object is neither rare nor pathological and does not always produce guilt feelings. It is perhaps a common, even universal, way of softening the loss of an important person. It can take a wide variety of forms besides the one Freud described.

A friend of mine attended his father's college and, like his father before him, got his degree with a minimum of reading, particularly of literature. He then landed a business-related job. Shortly after he graduated, his mother died. Almost at once he startled us all by enrolling in a Ph.D. program in literature and embarking on an intense study of Dickens and Shakespeare. His mother had been passionately fond of literature, particularly those two authors. He apparently made no conscious connection between his mother's death and his sudden new preoccupation.

Another friend asked a relative of his, on the eve of the relative's trip to Germany, to bring back a good Rolliflex camera. Since my friend had no interest in photography, it was a surprising request. His relative brought him the camera, and to my knowledge he never took a picture with it. Many years later that same friend returned from a vacation in Japan with an expensive Nikon. He explained to me that it seemed a shame to be there and not pick one up since they were less expensive in Japan. I don't think he took more than a handful of pictures with it. For many years it has gathered dust on the back of a closet shelf. Just before his relative's trip to Germany, my friend had been divorced by his first wife. She was, as you might have guessed, an enthusiastic photographer and the owner of a Rolliflex. My friend's trip to Japan was in part to help him get over his very recent separation from his second wife. She too was a photographer; her camera was a Nikon. Like my friend the

Shakespeare scholar, this friend made no conscious connection between his losses and his apparently inexplicable desire for two cameras.

In Chapter 4 we saw Freud's description of a young woman who considered that her mother and father conceiving a baby meant that she had lost her father. In response to this loss, the aspect of her father she chose to introject was his sexual interest in women. This then reinforced her homosexual orientation.

In "Mourning and Melancholia" Freud didn't discuss the effects of incomplete mourning, but those implications were not missed by writers who followed Freud. One of the most influential was the Boston psychoanalyst Erich Lindemann. Lindemann had long been interested in the subject of grief reaction, when, in 1943, a terrible accident filled his hospital with the dead, the dying, and the bereaved. On a Saturday night following a major football game, the crowded Coconut Grove restaurant burned to the ground. Nearly 500 people died. In the aftermath of that disaster Lindemann and his associates in the psychiatry department suddenly had a large number of bereaved people to try to help. Out of that experience came a highly influential paper, "Symptomatology and Management of Acute Grief."[5]

The main thrust of Lindemann's observations was that to liberate oneself from the pain and paralysis of acute grief it is necessary that the mourning process be completed, that the reality and the implications of the loss be deeply accepted. Absence of mourning or incomplete mourning puts the bereaved person in danger of depression, of interpersonal withdrawal, of loss of interest in life, and even of such physical problems as ulcerative colitis.

Mourning, as Freud observed, is extremely painful, and the intuitive response of many bereaved people is to try to minimize it or avoid it altogether. Friends and family often cooperate in this avoidance by trying to distract the person, saying things like, "Now, stop talking about her so much; it just makes you cry."

Many therapists, when confronted with a client who seems inexplicably depressed or withdrawn, or one who has certain intractable psychosomatic problems, will gently search the client's past for a loss that has not been adequately mourned. Upon finding such a loss, the therapist will consider it part of his or her job to encourage and support the mourning as an important part of the therapy.

Colin Murray Parkes,[6] a British psychoanalyst, has studied grief and bereavement extensively. His studies strongly support Lindemann's views on the necessity of mourning to liberate the bereaved from paralyzing grief and to enable them to go forward with their lives. Parkes points out how costly it is that our society (Europe and America) doesn't ritualize mourning and provide religious and institutional opportunities for it. Anthropologists G. Gorer[7] and E. Burgoine agree. They found that in Northern Europe and much of the United States, more than a little mourning is considered unseemly. Parkes believes that as a consequence the bereaved in our society fare significantly worse than those in societies that ritualize and encourage mourning. For example, the bereaved of a West Indian Christian sect called the Spiritual Baptists are supported in a mourning ritual that is characterized by community praying and fasting. Investigators report significant reduction of distress after such a ritual.

Gorer found in his survey that the social structure of contemporary Britain offers little help or guidance in the crises of misery and loneliness to which everyone is vulnerable. One cause of this, Gorer suggests, is the decline in formal religious belief and ritual. Parkes agrees, reporting that the English widows in his studies who avoided grieving did not engage in formal mourning, and he doubts that this would have happened in a society that had established expectations of the ritual expression of grief.[8]

A group of newly bereaved widows in New Providence, Bahamas, had better health and fewer psychological problems than the widows living in London. Burgoine, who did this study, attributes this to the overt expressions of grief that are expected and encouraged in the culture of New Providence.[9]

A study comparing reactions to the death of a close relative in Scottish and Swazi women found that the Swazi, who engage in extensive ritualized and socially supported mourning, showed more distress immediately after the death, but they were less troubled by guilt feelings a year later than were the Scottish widows.[10]

From Freud onward, those who have studied grief say that to liberate themselves, most bereaved people must mourn fully. This means in practice that the bereaved must

- allow themselves to cry;
- be willing to talk a good deal about the loss, the pain of the loss, and what they anticipate the loss will mean in their lives;
- be willing to talk about the lost person and about shared experiences with the lost person;

- be encouraged to talk about any anger they feel toward the lost person;
- be encouraged to express freely any guilt they feel toward the lost person, including the guilt over not having done enough to save him or her; and
- be given sympathetic support for all of the above.

Parkes adds to those suggestions a caution that might be paraphrased as, "Yes, but not too soon." His observations suggest that in the first hours or even days following the loss, a bereaved person needs support and comfort and is not yet ready to face the pain of mourning. He thus believes that funerals often come too soon. The pain must be let in gradually, he says, but it must be let in. Parkes's data strongly support Lindemann and others who observe that inadequate recovery from loss is caused by incomplete mourning. The analysts have taught us that we don't do ourselves or our friends a favor when we say, "Try not to think about her; it just makes you cry." This is a major contribution.

11

TRANSFERENCE

[T]ransference lies at the heart of psychoanalysis and was one of Freud's most central and profoundly creative discoveries. It is a powerful concept, speaking to the essence of the unconscious—the past hidden within the present—and of continuity—the present in continuum with the past.
   —E. A. Schwaber, *The Transference in Psychotherapy*

Freud's first collaborator was Joseph Breuer, a neurologist who was treating a young woman named Bertha Pappenheim. In Breuer and Freud's published account of the case,[1] her pseudonym was Ann O. Bertha was a very attractive and intelligent young woman suffering from a collection of distressing symptoms including a rigid paralysis of one arm, a severe nervous cough, aversion to drinking fluids, periods of disturbing hallucinations, and trouble speaking. In fact, for some time this native German speaker could speak only in English. Her symptoms had appeared when her father, whom she adored, had become mortally ill. She devoted all her time and energy to nursing him until her symptoms became so severe that she was forced to stop.

Breuer found the case fascinating. He described the case and the treatment to Freud, continuing to inform him as the treatment progressed. Breuer saw Bertha almost every day, often in her bedroom. The treatment that Breuer and Bertha jointly developed consisted of Breuer hypnotizing Bertha and suggesting she talk, beginning with words he had heard her mumble in states of hallucination and going on to speaking freely about whatever thoughts came into her mind. She called it "chimney sweeping." As Freud listened to Breuer's description of this intelligent and interesting woman he began to realize that Breuer was at least as fascinated with her as with the case.

One day Bertha told Breuer she was carrying his baby. There was no question in Freud's mind that Breuer's relationship with Bertha had been impeccably ethical. In fact, he shared Breuer's conviction that she was a virgin. The pregnancy turned out to have been entirely imagined by Bertha. Breuer's response was to stop the treatment immediately and leave town on a second honeymoon with his wife.

As Freud pondered this turn in Bertha's treatment, he realized that there was nothing remarkable about an engaging woman and a good-looking man becoming attracted to each other. What did seem remarkable to him was that Bertha had convinced herself that she was pregnant and about to deliver Breuer's baby.

The relationship Breuer and Bertha had established had stirred deep feelings and yearnings in both of them, feelings and yearnings of which they were not entirely aware. This was Freud's first intimation that a psychotherapeutic relationship could stir in both people a remarkable intensity, part of which, perhaps most of which, was unconscious. He also realized that the patient sometimes sees the therapist and their relationship through a lens distorted by unconscious forces. Later Freud became interested in the similar intensities and distortions that might develop in the therapist, but at first his attention was focused on the patient.

As he pondered these phenomena in his patients and in those of his colleagues, Freud decided that there were two unconscious forces at work. The first he called the ongoing power of the *template*. By this he meant that our earliest relationships form in our minds templates into which we attempt to fit all subsequent relationships. If I saw my father as severe and critical, in some part of my mind I will expect all older men in authority to be severe and critical. If the influence of the template is sufficiently strong and pervasive I may expect all men, perhaps all persons, to be this way. Similarly, if I saw my father as nurturing and supportive, I will expect to find those attributes in older male authorities that I meet along the way.

The second force was one we have already met: the repetition compulsion, that strange, very common need to replay old traumatic situations or old traumatic relationships. When the patient enters therapy, perhaps his or her father template causes him or her to see the therapist as severe and critical. Then the repetition compulsion may cause him or her to confirm that expectation by acting in ways calculated to irritate the therapist. Because these attitudes and expectations are "transferred" from the parent to the therapist, Freud called this tendency in therapy patients "transference." This turned out to be one of his most extraordinary insights.

The importance of this insight does not depend solely on its value to a therapist. Soon Freud came to realize that, like our tendency to replay old situations, our persistent expectations don't happen just in the therapy situation but everywhere, in all our relationships. Later in this chapter we will examine this ubiquity of the transference phenomenon, how it operates outside of therapy as well as inside, how it provides us all with a remarkable tool to deepen our self-understanding, and how it illuminates the ongoing vitality of psychodynamic theory.

Freud observed that the transference could take a variety of forms. For example, the patient could see the therapist as the critical father or the nurturing mother or a competitive sibling.

> My client Beverly was constantly suspicious of me. She didn't trust me to show up for appointments; she didn't believe my assurances of confidentiality; she doubted me when I said that I could understand a feeling she reported. Every therapist must earn the trust of each client, but this seemed extreme. Gradually I learned how this suspicion was being transferred to me from that originally stirred by her remarkably untrustworthy father. He would promise outings and then renege. He would reveal before her friends things she had assumed were family confidences. He had promised to support her college education and had flagrantly broken the promise.

Freud came to think that there were three categories of transference:[2]

- The *positive transference*, in which the patient's feelings for the therapist are primarily affection and trust.
- The *negative transference*, consisting primarily of hostility and suspicion.

- The *un-neutralized erotic transference,* in which the patient experiences insistent desire for sexual intimacy with the analyst.

Freud considered the positive transference "unobjectionable." It was what enabled the work of therapy to get done by providing the patient with confidence in the therapist and a feeling of being supported through painful and arduous parts of the journey. Freud advised the therapist to do nothing about positive transference. Just be grateful you've got it, he said. It makes your work possible. When I told my second analyst that I loved her, she remained silent. In those days that was considered good technique; it followed Freud's injunction to leave the positive transference alone.

The negative transference is a different story. It must be interpreted, Freud said, or else the patient's hostility and suspicion will make your work impossible. When I told my first analyst that I thought he was an incompetent fool, he suggested that unconsciously I was very angry at my father. However clumsily he did it, this too was considered good technique, although, as we'll soon see, modern analysts would respond quite differently.

Freud warned that the erotic transference might cause the analyst and patient serious trouble. It is not unusual for patients to be aware of erotic feelings for the analyst. Often they are merely a mild aspect of a positive transference and pose no difficulties. Like the negative transferences, these were classically interpreted as not "really" being about the analyst but rather about parental figures. However, if the erotic feelings were very insistent, and if interpretation failed to convert them to useful analytic exploration, they might stop the analysis in its tracks. In effect, the patient says, "I am no longer interested in the analysis; I just want intimate physical contact with you." Freud thought that if those feelings persisted in spite of the analyst's best efforts to convert them to analyzable material, there was nothing to do but refer the patient to another therapist.

In Freud's theory all positive feelings were expressions of libidinal energy, just as all negative feelings were expressions of destructive energy. One of the tasks faced by the ego is "neutralizing" that raw energy so that it is productive and socially acceptable. Neutralization refers to the conversion of raw libido into such emotions as affection, respect, and tender love. Neutralization of destructive energy means converting that energy into useful impulses such as competition, assertiveness, and playful aggression. One of the psychological bases for a successful life is adequate neutralization. An erotic transference so insistent that it destroys the analysis is the insufficiently neutralized expression of the same energy that creates the unobjectionable positive transference.

Freud began by looking at the phenomenon of transference as an interference with the true analytic work of uncovering unconscious feelings and fantasies. He saw himself as an archaeologist of the mind whose job was carefully to unearth the buried memories, to make conscious the previously unconscious feelings and memories that caused the patient trouble. Any transference other than a purely positive one that facilitated cooperation he viewed as a distraction and an impediment. However, relatively early in the development of psychoanalytic technique he began to see all transference as his ally, a troublesome ally to be sure, but an indispensable one.

Freud needed such an ally because of the frustration of his early hopes that the unconscious could readily be made conscious, thus curing the patient. He thought that he could accomplish that goal by discovering a particular unconscious memory or wish that was at the root of the problem and simply telling it to the patient. He quickly and sadly discovered that that was not enough, that a simple insight into the unconscious realms of the mind may indeed be necessary for cure, but it was certainly not sufficient. Often imparting such an insight to a patient caused no change at all in the patient's behavior or degree of suffering. Sometimes there would be an encouraging change in the patient that would prove discouragingly transitory. Freud was discovering that it was possible for a patient to "know" something intellectually without deeply knowing it. My analyst explained to me that I continually expected punishment in my adult life because I was unconsciously guilty about fancied childhood sins. It sounded persuasive; nevertheless, there was little change in my life. Even though she had made the connection conscious, it apparently had little effect on the unconscious part of my mind.

Ever since Freud made that frustrating discovery, the history of psychotherapy—all psychotherapy, not just psychoanalysis—can be seen as one attempt after another to discover what has to be added to insight to effect cure. Analysts refer to this something-that-must-be-added as "emotional working through," which means getting the insights to a place in the patient's mind where they can be used. Freud first hoped that the way to do this was by accumulating evidence, by showing the patient instance after instance of the impact of the unconscious fantasies. That's why psychoanalysis took so long. In my analysis I learned the multitude of ways this fantasy of my sinfulness affected me. It affected my work; my relationship with my girlfriend; and my relations with my teachers, with fellow students, with my landlord, and with my auto mechanic. I began to think that when psychoanalysis succeeded it did so by boring the symptom to death.

Freud's first major discovery about the doctor-patient relationship had come when he saw how much the nature of that relationship could impede or facilitate the progress of the treatment. Dentists or surgeons presumably need not concern themselves with your feelings about them. If you hold still or keep your mouth open they can do their work whether you like them or not. Freud had discovered how dramatically untrue this was of the psychotherapeutic relationship. Then he made his second major discovery about the relationship. Freud came to realize that troublesome though it might be, the transference provided him with his most powerful tool to effect the working through. He observed that the transference could become so strong that it produced what he called a "transference neurosis," meaning that the most significant of the patient's problems would manifest themselves in the relationship with the analyst.

> Alice was a sophisticated client who recognized early in our long course of therapy that there was significant undone work in her resolution of the Oedipus complex. She spoke freely of her childhood puzzlement over the nature of her father's affectionate contacts with her, knowing they made her uncomfortable, but not certain why. In her adult life she often found herself attracted to men who wanted her mainly for sex. Alice and I worked long and hard on her Oedipal fixation and its replays in her adult life. She understood both of these in excruciating detail; nonetheless, she continued the pattern. From time to time I asked her how

she felt about me and how she imagined I felt about her. She usually replied that it was too scary to look at. Then finally after many months, it came out hesitantly: She didn't trust me; she was convinced my interest in her was erotic, that she couldn't trust me to respect the appropriate boundaries of the therapeutic relationship, and that she needed to be on guard against me. I wouldn't be surprised if at some level of my consciousness she was right about the eros, if not about the danger to the boundaries. She was very attractive, and I can't imagine spending a lot of intimate time in the company of an attractive woman without some eros cropping up somewhere. But it was far from my conscious mind; I had my hands full just watching the store.

If this had been 1955 I would have assured her it wasn't I of whom she was afraid, it was her father. But it was not 1955, and the profession has come a long way since then. I told her how much I appreciated her courage in risking such a disclosure and that I could readily understand how frightening it would be to think that her therapist was not only attracted to her but perhaps had hopes of actually seducing her. I asked if she could tell me the cues she perceived. There was something about the way I greeted her that seemed more personal than how a therapist greets a client, she replied. Over several sessions she explored that at length, giving me specific instances. I said that I did understand that my behaving so "personal" to her could make her wonder about my motives. Many of our sessions during the next weeks included discussion of these perceptions and the ensuing feelings. From time to time I said I thought her perception of my warmth was certainly accurate but that I was not aware of having the feelings she feared I was having. However, I added, we both had developed a great respect for the unconscious.

Finally I suggested that although her interpretation of my warmth was certainly plausible it was not the only possible interpretation. My warmth might just represent a non-erotic interest and affection. She agreed that seemed possible. I asked her if she would be willing to look for possible reasons for having chosen the eros-and-seduction interpretation. She burst out laughing, and said, "I can't imagine; can you?"

Her therapy continued for some time after that, but her life began to change. We explored at length the possibility that she not only feared my sexual interest in her, which she certainly did, but that at a deeper level she also desired it. The reader will remember Freud's admonition that a strong fear may often conceal a wish.

Eventually Alice found an unattached man and fell in love. I wish I could say that working through the insights in the transference always works this way. I'm afraid it sometimes doesn't. But often it works as Freud said it did:

It is on the field [of transference] that the victory must be won—the victory whose expression is the permanent cure of the neurosis. It cannot be disputed that controlling the phenomena of transference presents the psychoanalyst with the greatest difficulties. But it should not be forgotten that it is precisely they that do us the inestimable service of making the patient's hidden and forgotten erotic impulses immediate and manifest. For when all is said and done, it is impossible to destroy anyone *in absentia* or *in effigie*.[3]

Merton Gill and Contemporary
Transference Analysis

Freud was convinced that the secret to a cure was recovering buried impulses and fantasies from their repression. The value of working through insights in the transference, he suspected, was that the realizations about distortions in the therapeutic relationship would be significantly more convincing to the patient than those about events and relationships outside the therapeutic situation. In his last published work he wrote: *"A patient never forgets again what he has experienced in the form of transference; it carries a greater force of conviction than anything he can acquire in other ways."*[4] The emphasis was on the cognitive realization.

Freud believed that the analyst could and should detect the ways in which the patient's view of the therapist was distorted by the templates. By demonstrating these distortions the analyst could teach the patient lasting lessons about the patient's destructively distorted perceptions. However, there are problems with this point of view.

When my client tells me that I am uptight and defensive, I think to myself, "Ah, she must have had a defensive father." When she tells me she appreciates how hard working and dedicated I am, I think to myself, "Yes, that's a realistic picture of me." You see the problem: The therapist is in no position to decide which of the client's responses are realistic and which "distorted." When psychoanalysts finally realized that, they had at last discovered what any first-year graduate student in philosophy or high-energy physics could have told them: "Reality" is a very tricky concept to define.

One of Freud's most important followers, the American psychoanalyst Merton Gill (1914–1994), offered a creative and satisfying solution: Each of us views interpersonal interactions through the lens of our unconscious fantasies, through the lens of the idiosyncratic principles by which we have learned to organize experience. Interpersonal stimuli are very likely to be ambiguous, lending themselves to multiple interpretations. How we choose among those interpretations is determined by our organizing principles, by our templates. That is true not only of the client but of the therapist as well.

Gill[5] has had a great impact on the practice of psychoanalysis and on the other forms of dynamic psychotherapy as well. There are today few practicing dynamic therapists not influenced by Gill and his descendants.

Most therapists have given up the notion that they are in a position to judge which of the client's perceptions are realistic and which are distorted. All of these perceptions are realistic to some extent and all are shaped to some extent by the templates. The word "transference" had originally referred to the perceptions and reactions of the client that the therapist thought to be distorted. That definition was no longer serviceable once psychoanalysts had abandoned the conviction that they had special insights into what was real. Several attempts have been made to redefine transference. It seems most useful simply to consider that since we cannot presume to distinguish "realistic" from "distorted," and since we acknowledge that all our interpersonal perceptions are shaped in part by the templates, we give the name transference to *all* feelings, thoughts, perceptions, and judgments the client has about the therapist.

Gill also proposed how transference might be employed in the service of the client. He noted that, as we saw in Chapter 2, repressed material seeks expression. He further noted that Freud had demonstrated that the therapeutic situation is an ideal outlet for this material. Gill proposed, then, that the primary therapeutic factor in the clinical relationship was the opportunity to re-experience the ancient buried impulses and fantasies in the transference, to express them to the therapist, and to have them be met with a significantly different response than they had been met with originally. The patient's maladaptive beliefs and attitudes were acquired in interpersonal interaction, Gill reasoned, and thus they must be changed in that same context.

To Gill it would not have been enough for me to have explained to Alice that her fear of me was a distorted replay of her fear of her father, or that under her fear resided a wish for him to be attracted to her. To Gill my first task was to acknowledge her fear of me as real and important and to encourage her to explore it in detail, including the cues she detected in me. Similarly, it would have been important to Gill that I make it safe for her to tell me of the underlying wish, the wish that I be attracted to her. Then, Gill says, it would have been possible and necessary to help her explore the ancient roots of her fear and her wish.

As can be seen in the quote about destroying anyone in absentia or in effigy, Freud was working his way toward this position. It was Gill, however, who actually moved the technique of transference analysis an important and influential step forward.

Heinz Kohut and the Selfobject Transference

An equally important follower of Freud in the realm of understanding transference was Heinz Kohut (1913–1981). Of the many valuable innovations in psychoanalysis Kohut made, the one that concerns us here is his description of the "selfobject" transference, the hope that here at last is the parent for whom I have been hoping and waiting.[6]

This is Kohut's notion of the selfobject: Soon after birth the infant and child becomes occupied with three crucial unconscious questions, questions that in a healthy, loving home are answered positively by the parents. First, am I a lovable person who is welcome here? Someone, often mother, like the mirror in *Snow White,* sends her infant the message that he or she is the fairest and most wonderful of them all. That response is the one that forever establishes the child's self-esteem.

Somewhat later comes the second question: How can a small, inexperienced being like me cope with this overwhelming world and these overwhelming feelings? This question is answered by the child learning that one or both of the parents is calm, confident, and competent. It is not yet necessary that the child be able to cope; the capable parent or parents will take care of things while the child becomes stronger and more experienced. This establishes an important sense of security.

Finally, the third question is: Am I comfortably like other people and therefore acceptable, or am I weird and unacceptable? When parents invite the child to share adult activities the child hears the message, all the more powerful for being unspoken, "I'm not weird; I'm like mommy or daddy."

Kohut believed that the fate of these needs for love and security was a crucial determinant of the child's subsequent mental health. If these needs are adequately met (Kohut didn't think that happened often) the child grows into a healthy adolescent ready to take on the Oedipus complex successfully, and then into a healthy adult. If these needs are not adequately met, the person is a candidate for psychotherapy. Those unmet needs will remain a permanent, unconscious driving force in that person's life. Like the template, they will manifest themselves at every opportunity.

Freud taught us that transference was a replay of early relationships. I unconsciously expect people to be the way they were in my childhood, and I act in ways calculated to fulfill that prophecy. Kohut recognized that transference-as-replay certainly happens, but he described another form transference can take: transference as the *hope for something better* than the original relationships. If I had a critical father, my unconscious template will cause me to see my analyst as critical. But the unconscious wish to satisfy the old need may also cause me to see him as the warm, loving father I didn't have and always wanted. In Kohut's vocabulary, I am now seeing the therapist as the loving, validating *selfobject* that I so needed and didn't get. Kohut called this the "selfobject transference."

Since the advent of Kohut's contributions, psychoanalysts have recognized these two types of transference. Robert Stolorow and his colleagues[7] teach that it is likely the client will oscillate between these two types of transference. When the therapist is empathically tuned to the client, Stolorow says, the client will experience a selfobject transference. When the transference shifts to an ancient template, Stolorow advises the therapist to suspect that he or she has been guilty of an empathic failure. When that failure is explored and rectified, the transference will resume its selfobject form.

The replay transference heals by allowing the client to work through the ancient wounds. The selfobject transference heals by providing the therapist with opportunities to recognize and empathize with the client's long-standing, unconscious hunger for nurturance, support, and validation.

Transference in Everyday Life

Originally it seemed to Freud that transference was a phenomenon found primarily in the therapy situation. He soon came to realize that, on the contrary, it was everywhere. In all of our significant relationships, and a fair number of our trivial ones, wherever we go we are ceaselessly replaying some aspect of our early lives. We do it in our friendships, our business relationships, our love affairs, and particularly in our relationships with authority figures. An appreciation and understanding of transference is necessary for therapists. But for all of us, such understanding adds a rich perception to the design of our lives.

That design might be thought of as poetic, or more accurately, as musical. The composers of the eighteenth century employed a musical form called the sonata. The first movements of Beethoven's and Mozart's symphonies are examples. In the sonata form all of the themes of the movement appear at the beginning. The rest of the movement consists of the composer developing these themes, creating variations on them, and recapitulating them. It is a powerful design, and perhaps one of the reasons the music of that period is apparently going to be played forever. We might think of our lives as sonatas. All the relationship themes appear at the beginning, and the rest of our lives consist of our discovering variations, developments, and recapitulations of those themes.

Kohut suggested that, like the replay transferences, the self-object transferences also appear in all aspects of our lives. Even those who had their selfobject needs well met in childhood continue, throughout their lives, to seek others who will validate and inspire them. Those of us whose needs were not so well met do this even more energetically.

When I was an undergraduate, I usually sat in a lecture hall so large that I was far away from most professors and thus didn't have much of a feeling for or impression of them. I'm sure that didn't stop me from continual transference reactions, but their conscious manifestations seemed more amusing than important. Graduate school was something very different. I was in close contact with my professors, and their authority over me seemed practically unlimited. If I thought I detected in a professor the slightest sign of disapproval or even lack of interest, I was certain my career and I were in serious trouble. You can imagine how I had perceived my relationship with my father. On the other hand, if a professor seemed warm or interested in me, I quickly developed fantasies of earning his admiration and becoming his disciple. This is a typical selfobject transference, the hope for something better than the original relationship.

Understanding and appreciating the power of transference in everyday life gives us greatly increased understanding and appreciation of the unconscious forces acting on us and on the people around us.

Countertransference

We have seen that Freud and his followers came to believe that transference is a phenomenon common to everyone. That must certainly include therapists, and it must certainly include the relationship the therapist has with the client. The technical word for the therapist's reactions is *countertransference*. How this concept has been seen by psychoanalysts has a long history. Originally it was thought, or perhaps hoped, that analysts were so thoroughly analyzed and so professional that they would have no perceptions of the client but purely realistic ones and no responses to the vagaries of the client's transference but thoroughly appropriate ones. Freud recognized that occasionally some unconscious derivative would break through the therapist's professionalism and produce an inappropriate response. He called this response "countertransference," and he saw it as nothing but an obstacle to be removed. He hoped that if the therapist could not analyze it away by self-scrutiny, he or she would seek consultation or even further analysis.

That was the beginning of a long journey. Analysts began to wonder if it really were possible for anyone to be that thoroughly analyzed. Countertransference was recognized to be inevitable and continuous. By 1950 it was seen as not only inevitable but actually useful. By the 1960s it was seen as indispensable.

We have seen that analysts have finally and blessedly given up the belief that they could distinguish between real and distorted. Inevitably that change dramatically altered the view of countertransference. From this perspective we might define countertransference as *all* the feelings, thoughts, and perceptions the therapist has about the client. We can see why it's indispensable; all empathy, for example, begins with countertransference.

Intersubjectivity

Once the elusiveness of reality has been acknowledged, the entire picture of the therapeutic relationship changes. Originally it was confidently believed that a clear-sighted person was treating someone whose neurosis clouded his or her vision. Now it seems that a more accurate, and certainly more modest, picture is that each of the two people is viewing the actuality of the other through the lens of his or her unique organizing principles. Neither is distorting; neither is in touch with some absolute reality. This is not to say that the relationship is now seen as *symmetrical;* both are there in service of the client. But no longer is it believed that therapists' perceptions, particularly their *self-*perceptions, are more accurate than those of their clients.

Just as physicists had learned the extent of the observer's impact on the observed, analysts are now learning what an enormous impact the organizing principles, often the *unconscious* organizing principles, of the therapist have on the client. This perspective has come to be known as "intersubjective," meaning that the emerging understanding of the client is jointly shaped by the subjectivities of client and therapist. It hardly seems meaningful to use the term countertransference any more, because it is now clear that we are dealing with two sets of transferences.

Had my therapy with Alice occurred 25 years ago I would not even have considered it possible that she was indeed detecting unconscious erotic feelings in me. Had I been *aware* of conscious desire for her, I would have considered it regrettable countertransference and sought consultation. Had I not been aware of erotic feelings, I would have assumed that her perception was entirely determined by her Oedipal feelings, and not at all by anything going on in me. But therapists who write from an intersubjective perspective—Robert Stolorow and his collaborators,[8] Irwin Hoffman,[9] Stephen Mitchell,[10] and Lew Aron[11] to name only a few—have opened our eyes to the importance of taking seriously the client's perception of the therapist.

This raises the question of a therapist's self-disclosure. The classic psychoanalytic position was clear: The therapist *never* reveals his or her feelings. Writers on intersubjectivity have re-opened the question. It is now a central frontier issue and very controversial, although beyond the scope of this book.

The theory of transference, broadly conceived, teaches us that to each of our interpersonal encounters we bring our buried history of wishes, fears, and psychic traumas. The power of the unconscious to influence our perceptions of and reactions to each other, whether in therapy or in life, is one of Freud's most valuable and illuminating discoveries.

12

CONCLUSION

Inscribed on the Oracle at Delphi are the words, "Know Thyself."
That is easier said than done. Though the goal is always beyond
reach, the search for it is the supreme journey, for along the way you
will find the poetry of your soul.

Freud's contribution to our self-understanding was a feat of undeniable genius. Yet not all of his theoretical adventures were successful. It seems the one that particularly disappointed him was psychoanalytic therapy. By the end of his life he had grave doubts about the therapeutic efficacy of psychoanalysis as it was then practiced. During Freud's lifetime, and for at least three decades after his death, psychoanalysis may well have been the best possible postgraduate education a person could have, but it was not as helpful in alleviating life's problems as Freud hoped it would be.

But the psychodynamic therapy he invented and launched has assumed many more shapes than the original psychoanalysis and, beginning with the major advances of the 1960s and 1970s, has been steadily improved.

The original formulation—neurotic symptoms are always the expression of repressed sexual impulses—has been greatly expanded to make room for any number of possible unconscious conflicts. Destructive injunctions from the original caretakers, learned and then repressed, might be about sex. They might also be about the expression, or merely the feeling, of anger. One might learn early that he or she is not lovable or not capable of handling the exigencies of life. All of these conflicts can give rise to problems in living. This expanded awareness has made possible more effective therapy.

Psychodynamic therapists now understand that the healing power of the therapeutic relationship itself is as great as the power of bringing unconscious forces to the surface. Understanding how these work together has produced a quantum leap in therapeutic effectiveness.

The classic therapist's stance was often restrained and reticent. Contemporary therapists now permit themselves a good deal more self-disclosure, as well as a more relaxed, friendly relationship with their clients. These freedoms add to the therapeutic power of psychodynamic treatment.

For those who can afford it, the classic psychoanalytic arrangements—four or five sessions a week for several years—is still practiced, and with far more sophistication than in the early days. A number of more modest, but very effective, psychodynamic techniques have come from Freud's original insights, and these are being steadily improved. I venture to guess that were Freud to return, he would be surprised and pleased that his followers have taken the therapeutic power of psychodynamic therapy far beyond his gloomy expectations.

It is remarkable that a single man was originally responsible for all of the forms of depth therapy being practiced in the world today. Depth therapy is the attempt to convert the most important unconscious forces from enemies into allies. There have been many divisions of this field and many innovators. Within the mainstream of Freudian psychoanalysis there are relational therapists,[1] self psychologists,[2] and object-relations therapists.[3] The followers of C. G. Jung[4] and Alfred Adler[5] have explored territory far from Freud's. But the methods of all of them grew out of Freud's stunning original insights. Yet, when the history of our time is written, it may not be Freud's therapeutic method that will constitute the most important part of his legacy.

This book began by quoting Joseph Campbell:

[T]he human kingdom, beneath the floor of the comparatively neat little dwelling that we call our consciousness, goes down into unsuspected Aladdin caves. There not only jewels but also dangerous jinn abide: the inconvenient or resisted psychological powers that we have not thought or dared to integrate into our lives.[6]

Freud ventured into those caves, inviting us to follow. Some of those who have followed might have made that journey hoping that the underworld offers teachings that might reduce their pain and bewilderment. Others might be seeking to improve their skills as helpers. Still others might see that journey as a way of discovering the beauty and poetry, including the dark poetry, of life's complexity. But whatever the reason, anyone who has made that journey, even a small part of that journey, is unlikely ever to be the same.

I noted early in this book the source of Freud's insights. I observed that it is very likely no one in human history had listened to another person the way Freud listened to his patients, hour after hour, day after day, year after year. And probably no one

before him had ever gone to such lengths to encourage the
speaker to abandon censorship. It is not surprising that he
heard things no one had heard before, and that he learned
things about mental and emotional life that no one before had
suspected.

Perhaps the most important thing Freud contributed to our
understanding of ourselves was that the greatest part of mental
and emotional life is hidden, that consciousness is a small part
of the human mind. Motives are concealed, feelings are buried,
conflicting forces struggle out of sight.

Freud also added the following insights to our self-understanding:

- A great deal of our inner life is designed to protect us
  from anxiety, guilt, and shame, and the defense mechanisms we use to do so are often seriously maladaptive.
  They may end by causing far more suffering than
  would the warded-off feelings and impulses. Although
  inadequate defenses can lead to chaos, too much or
  too rigid defense leads to an inhibited and distorted
  life.
- Humans have a puzzling unconscious compulsion to
  repeat early painful experiences, to repeat them over
  and over, and to teach other people to play the necessary complementary roles in that repetition.
- Relationship difficulties in childhood are likely to have
  lasting impact. Particularly important are those sur-
  rounding the Oedipus complex and its resolution.
- Unconscious guilt can have a powerful effect on our
  lives.
- There is meaningful, revealing sense to dreams.

- Our first relationships make an enduring impression and color our view of subsequent ones, that is, transference accompanies us everywhere.

Those who study the European Renaissance often cite three thinkers as having shaken human self-image so profoundly that it made possible such miracles as Shakespeare's plays. Copernicus broke the news that we are not at the center of the universe and therefore not any more special to God than any of the other divine creations. Montaigne argued persuasively that far from being junior angels, we are, by measure of grace, morality, and beauty, somewhere below the animals in the cosmic hierarchy. Machiavelli pointed out that we are not actually governed by divine right, by kings serving faithfully as God's stewards, but rather by chicanery and manipulation.

In the present age, who shakes our confidence that we know ourselves and our world? Darwin, Marx, and Einstein would have to be candidates for such a list. But it would be hard to imagine an intellectual history of the last century that did not also prominently include Freud, who taught us to be skeptical about everything we think we know and endlessly curious about what else we might really know.

NOTES

Preface

1. B. Bettelheim, *Freud and Man's Soul* (New York: Alfred A. Knopf, 1983), p. 4.

Chapter One

1. J. Lear, *Open Minded.* (Cambridge: Harvard University Press, 1998), p. 18.

2. Ibid., p. 28.

3. R. D. Stolorow, B. Brandschaft, and G. E. Atwood, *Psychoanalytic Treatment: An Intersubjective Approach* (Hillsdale, N.J.: Analytic Press, 1987), p. 65.

Chapter Two

1. S. Freud, *Introductory Lectures,* vol. 15 of *The Standard Edition of the Complete Psychological Works of Sigmund Freud* (London: Hogarth, 1915), p. 57.

2. Freud, *Introductory Lectures,* p. 295.

3. S. Freud, *The Ego and the Id,* vol. 19 of *The Standard Edition of the Complete Psychological Works of Sigmund Freud* (London: Hogarth, 1923), p. 25.

4. Freud, *Introductory Lectures,* p. 122.

5. Ibid., p. 124.

6. Ibid., p. 264.

7. S. Freud, *The Psychopathology of Everyday Life,* vol. 6 of *The Standard Edition of the Complete Psychological Works of Sigmund Freud* (London: Hogarth, 1901).

8. Ibid., p. 9.

9. S. Freud, *Three Essays on Sexuality,* vol. 7 of *The Standard Edition of the Complete Psychological Works of Sigmund Freud* (London: Hogarth, 1905), p. 125.

Chapter Three

1. S. Freud, "Three Essays on Sexuality," in vol. 7 of *The Standard Edition of the Complete Psychological Works of Sigmund Freud* (London: Hogarth, 1905), p. 187.

2. S. Freud, "A Case of Hysteria," in vol. 7 of *The Standard Edition of the Complete Psychological Works of Sigmund Freud* (London: Hogarth, 1905), p. 51.

3. S. Freud, *Introductory Lectures,* vol. 16 of *The Standard Edition of the Complete Psychological Works of Sigmund Freud* (London: Hogarth, 1915), p. 341.

Chapter Four

1. S. Freud, *The Interpretation of Dreams,* vol. 4 of *The Standard Edition of the Complete Psychological Works of Sigmund Freud* (London: Hogarth, 1900), p. 261.

2. G. Lindzey, "Some Remarks Concerning Incest, the Incest Taboo, and Psychoanalytic Theory," *American Psychologist* 22, no. 12 (1967): 1051.

3. A. W. Johnson and D. Price-Williams, *Oedipus Ubiquitous* (Stanford, Calif.: Stanford University Press, 1966), p. 98.

4. Ibid., p. 141.

5. Ibid., p. 153.

6. J. M. Masson, *The Assault on Truth: Freud's Suppression of the Seduction Theory* (New York: Farrar, Straus & Giroux, 1984).

7. R. Ofshe and E. Watters, *Making Monsters: False Memories, Psychotherapy, and Sexual Hysteria* (Berkeley: University of California Press, 1996).

8. J. Benjamin, *The Bonds of Love* (New York: Pantheon Books, 1988).

9. N. Chodorow, *The Reproduction of Mothering* (Berkeley: University of California Press, 1978).

10. M. S. Mahler, F. Pine, and A. Bergman, *The Psychological Birth of the Human Infant* (New York: Basic Books, 1975).

11. J. W. M. Whiting, R. Kluckhohn, and A. Anthony, "The Function of Male Initiation Rites at Puberty," in E. E. Maccoby, T. M. Newcomb, and E. L. Hartley, eds., *Readings in Social Psychology* (New York: Holt, 1958).

12. N. Chodorow, *The Reproduction of Mothering* (Berkeley: University of California Press, 1978), p. 133.

13. Benjamin, *Bonds of Love*.

14. Ibid., p. 111.

15. Freud, *Interpretation of Dreams*, p. 265.

Chapter Five

1. S. Freud, *Beyond the Pleasure Principle*, vol. 18 of *The Standard Edition of the Complete Psychological Works of Sigmund Freud* (London: Hogarth, 1920), p. 22.

2. Ibid., p. 7.

3. S. Freud, *Civilization and Its Discontents*, vol. 21 of *The Standard Edition of the Complete Psychological Works of Sigmund Freud* (London: Hogarth, 1930) pp. 118–119.

Chapter Six

1. S. Freud, *Introductory Lectures*, vol. 16 of *The Standard Edition of the Complete Psychological Works of Sigmund Freud* (London: Hogarth, 1915), p. 401.

2. S. Freud, *Inhibition, Symptom, and Anxiety*, vol. 20 of *The Standard Edition of the Complete Psychological Works of Sigmund Freud* (London: Hogarth, 1926), p. 75.

3. S. Freud, *Analysis of a Phobia in a Five-Year-Old Boy,* vol. 10 of *The Standard Edition of the Complete Psychological Works of Sigmund Freud* (London: Hogarth, 1909), p. 1.

4. J. Wolpe, *Psychotherapy by Reciprocal Inhibition* (Stanford, Calif.: Stanford University Press, 1958).

Chapter Seven

1. A. Freud, *Ego and the Mechanisms of Defense* (New York: International Universities Press, 1936).

2. M. Solomon, *Beethoven* (New York: Schirmer Books, 1977).

3. A. Freud, *Ego and the Mechanisms of Defense,* p. 117.

4. N. McWilliams, *Psychoanalytic Diagnosis* (New York: Guilford Press, 1994), p. 109.

5. B. Bettelheim, *The Informed Heart* (New York: Avon Books, 1960), p. 170.

6. A. Freud, *Ego and the Mechanisms of Defense,* pp. 48–50.

7. Ibid. p. 47.

Chapter Eight

1. Thomas of Celano, *Francis of Assisi* (New York: New City Press, 1999), p. 221.

2. S. Freud, *Civilization and Its Discontents,* vol. 21 of *The Standard Edition of the Complete Psychological Works of Sigmund Freud* (London: Hogarth, 1930), pp. 127–128.

3. S. Freud, " 'Civilized' Sexual Morality and Modern Nervous Illness," in vol. 9 of *The Standard Edition of the Complete Psychological Works of Sigmund Freud* (London: Hogarth, 1908), p. 177.

Chapter Nine

1. S. Freud, *The Interpretation of Dreams*, vols. 4 and 5 of *The Standard Edition of the Complete Psychological Works of Sigmund Freud* (London: Hogarth, 1900).

2. Ibid., p. 123.

3. Ibid., p. 355.

4. P. Lippman, "Dreams and Psychoanalysis: A Love-Hate Story." *Psychoanalytic Psychology* 17, no. 4 (2000): 627–650.

5. M. M. Gill, *The Analysis of Transference*, vol. 1 (New York: International Universities Press, 1982).

6. H. Kohut, *How Does Analysis Cure?* (Chicago: University of Chicago Press, 1984).

7. C. G. Jung, *The Archetypes and the Collective Unconscious,* vol. 9, part 1 of *The Collected Works* (Princeton: Princeton University Press, 1934).

Chapter Ten

1. S. Freud, "Mourning and Melancholia," in vol. 14 of *The Standard Edition of the Complete Psychological Works of Sigmund Freud* (London: Hogarth, 1917), p. 237.

2. Ibid., p. 244.

3. S. Freud, "The Ego and the Id," in vol. 19 of *The Standard Edition of the Complete Psychological Works of Sigmund Freud* (London: Hogarth, 1923), p. 3.

4. J. E. Baker, "Mourning and the Transformation of Object Relationships," *Psychoanalytic Psychology* 18, no. 1 (2001): 55–73.

5. E. Lindemann, "Symptomatology and Management of Acute Grief," *American Journal of Psychology* 101 (1944): 141–148.

6. C. M. Parkes, *Bereavement: Studies of Grief in Adult Life,* 3rd ed. (Madison, Conn.: International Universities Press, 1996).

7. G. Gorer, *Death, Grief, and Mourning in Contemporary Britain* (London: Cresset, 1965).

8. Ibid.; Parkes, *Bereavement,* p. 151.

9. E. Burgoine, A Cross-Cultural Comparison of Bereavement Among Widows in New Providence, Bahamas and London, England. Paper presented at the International Conference on Grief and Bereavement in Contemporary Society, London, England, July 12–15, 1988.

10. D. M. Lovell, G. Hemmings, and A. D. Hill, "Bereavement Reactions of Female Scots and Swazis: A Preliminary Comparison," *British Journal of Medical Psychology* 66, no. 3 (1993): 259–274.

Chapter Eleven

1. J. Breuer and S. Freud, *Studies in Hysteria,* vol. 2 of *The Standard Edition of the Complete Psychological Works of Sigmund Freud* (London: Hogarth, 1885), p. 1.

2. S. Freud, *The Dynamics of Transference,* vol. 12 of *The Standard Edition of the Complete Psychological Works of Sigmund Freud* (London: Hogarth, 1912), p. 99.

3. Ibid., p. 108.

4. S. Freud, *An Outline of Psychoanalysis,* vol. 23 of *The Standard Edition of the Complete Psychological Works of Sigmund Freud* (London: Hogarth, 1940), p. 177.

5. M. M. Gill, *The Analysis of Transference* (New York: International Universities Press, 1982).

6. H. Kohut, *The Restoration of the Self* (New York: International Universities Press, 1977); H. Kohut, *How Does Analysis Cure?* (Chicago: University of Chicago Press, 1984).

7. R. D. Stolorow, B. Brandschaft, and G. E. Atwood, *Psychoanalytic Treatment: An Intersubjective Approach* (Hillsdale, N.J.: Analytic Press, 1987).

8. R. D. Stolorow, G. E. Atwood, and B. Brandschaft, *The Intersubjective Perspective* (Hillsdale, N.J.: Analytic Press, 1994).

9. I. Hoffman, *Ritual and Spontaneity in the Psychoanalytic Process* (Hillsdale, N.J.: Analytic Press, 1998).

10. S. A. Mitchell, *Influence and Autonomy in Psychoanalysis* (Hillsdale, N.J.: Analytic Press, 1997).

11. L. Aron, *A Meeting of Minds: Mutuality in Psychoanalysis* (Hillsdale, N.J.: Analytic Press, 1996).

Chapter Twelve

1. S. A. Mitchell, *Relational Concepts in Psychoanalysis: An Integration* (Cambridge, Mass.: Harvard University Press, 1988).

2. H. Kohut, *How Does Analysis Cure?* (Chicago: University of Chicago Press, 1984).

3. J. R. Greenberg and S. A. Mitchell, *Object Relations in Psychoanalytic Theory* (Cambridge: Harvard University Press, 1983).

4. C. G. Jung, *Modern Man in Search of a Soul* (New York: Harcourt Brace, 1993).

5. A. Adler, *Social Interest: A Challenge to Mankind* (New York: Capricorn, 1929).

6. J. Campbell, *The Hero with a Thousand Faces* (Princeton, N.J.: Princeton University Press, 1949), p. 8.

BIBLIOGRAPHY

By and About Freud

Bettelheim, Bruno. *Freud and Man's Soul.* New York: Alfred A. Knopf, 1983.

Breuer, J., and S. Freud. *Studies in Hysteria.* Vol. 2 of *The Standard Edition of the Complete Psychological Works of Sigmund Freud.* London: Hogarth, 1885.

Freud, Anna. The *Ego and the Mechanisms of Defense.* New York: International Universities Press, 1936.

Freud, Sigmund. *Analysis of a Phobia in a Five-Year-Old Boy.* Vol. 10 of *The Standard Edition of the Complete Psychological Works of Sigmund Freud.* London: Hogarth, 1909.

_____. *Beyond the Pleasure Principle.* Vol. 18 of *The Standard Edition of the Complete Psychological Works of Sigmund Freud.* London: Hogarth, 1920.

_____. *Civilization and Its Discontents.* Vol. 21 of *The Standard Edition of the Complete Psychological Works of Sigmund Freud.* London: Hogarth, 1930.

_____. *"Civilized" Sexual Morality and Modern Nervous Illness.* Vol. 9 of *The Standard Edition of the Complete Psychological Works of Sigmund Freud.* London: Hogarth, 1908.

_____. *The Dynamics of Transference,* Vol. 12 of *The Standard Edition of the Complete Psychological Works of Sigmund Freud.* London: Hogarth, 1912.

_____. The *Ego and the Id*. Vol. 19 of *The Standard Edition of the Complete Psycological Works of Sigmund Freud*. London: Hogarth, 1923.

_____. *Five Lectures on Psychoanalysis*. Vol. 11 of *The Standard Edition of the Complete Psychological Works of Sigmund Freud*. London: Hogarth, 1910.

_____. *Inhibition, Symptom, and Anxiety*. Vol. 20 of *The Standard Edition of the Complete Psychological Works of Sigmund Freud*. London: Hogarth, 1926.

_____. *The Interpretation of Dreams*. Vols. 4 and 5 of *The Standard Edition of the Complete Psychological Works of Sigmund Freud*. London: Hogarth, 1900.

_____. *Introductory Lectures*. Vols. 15 and 16 of *The Standard Edition of the Complete Psychological Works of Sigmund Freud*. London: Hogarth, 1915.

_____. *An Outline of Psychoanalysis*. Vol. 23 of *The Standard Edition of the Complete Psychological Works of Sigmund Freud*. London: Hogarth, 1940.

_____. *The Psychopathology of Everyday Life*. Vol. 6 of *The Standard Edition of the Complete Psychological Works of Sigmund Freud*. London: Hogarth, 1901.

_____. *Three Essays on Sexuality*. Vol. 7 of *The Standard Edition of the Complete Psychological Works of Sigmund Freud*. London: Hogarth, 1905.

Lear, Jonathan. *Open Minded*. Cambridge: Harvard University Press, 1998.

Madison, P. *Freud's Concept of Repression and Defense*. Minneapolis: University of Minneapolis Press, 1961.

Masson, J. M. *The Assault on Truth: Freud's Suppression of the Seduction Theory*. New York: Farrar, Straus & Giroux, 1984.

Relational Psychoanalysis

Aron, Lewis. *A Meeting of Minds: Mutuality in Psychoanalysis*. Hillsdale, N.J.: The Analytic Press, 1996.

Gill, Merton. *The Analysis of Transference*. New York: International Universities Press, 1982.

_____. *Psychoanalysis in Transition.* Hillsdale, N.J.: Analytic Press, 1994.

Hoffman, Irwin. *Ritual and Spontaneity in the Psychoanalytic Process.* Hillsdale, N.J.: Analytic Press, 1998.

Mitchell, Stephen. *Influence and Autonomy in Psychoanalysis.* Hillsdale, N.J.: Analytic Press, 1997.

Stolorow, R. D., B. Brandschaft, and G. E. Atwood. *Psychoanalytic Treatment: An Intersubjective Approach.* Hillsdale, N.J.: Analytic Press, 1987.

Stolorow, Robert, George Atwood, and Bernard Brandschaft. *The Intersubjective Perspective.* Hillsdale, N.J.: Analytic Press, 1994.

Teicholz, Judith Guss. *Kohut, Loewald, and the Postmoderns.* Hillsdale, N.J.: Analytic Press, 1999.

Object Relations

Greenberg, J. R., and S. A. Mitchell. *Object Relations in Psychoanalytic Theory.* Cambridge: Harvard University Press, 1983.

Kohut's Self Psychology

Kohut, Heinz. *How Does Analysis Cure?* Chicago: University of Chicago Press, 1984.

Wolf, Ernest. *Treating the Self.* New York: Guilford Press, 1988.

General

Adler, A. *Social Interest: A Challenge to Mankind.* New York: Capricorn, 1929.

Benjamin, J. *The Bonds of Love.* New York: Pantheon Books, 1988.

Campbell, Joseph. *The Hero with a Thousand Faces.* Princeton, N.J.: Princeton University Press, 1949.

Chodorow, N. *The Reproduction of Mothering.* Berkeley: University of California Press, 1978.

Johnson, A. W., and D. Price-Williams. *Oedipus Ubiquitous.* Stanford, Calif.: Stanford University Press, 1966.

Jung, C. G. *Modern Man in Search of a Soul.* New York: Harcourt Brace, 1993.

Mahler, M. S., F. Pine, and A. Bergman. *The Psychological Birth of the Human Infant.* New York: Basic Books, 1975.

McWilliams, Nancy. *Psychoanalytic Diagnosis.* New York: Guilford Press, 1994.

Ofshe, R., and E. Watters. *Making Monsters: False Memories, Psychotherapy, and Sexual Hysteria.* Berkeley: University of California Press, 1996.

Schwaber, E. A. *The Transference in Psychotherapy.* New York: International Universities Press, 1985.

Wolpe, J. *Psychotherapy by Reciprocal Inhibition.* Stanford, Calif.: Stanford University Press, 1958.

INDEX

Addiction, 99–101

Adolescence: and defense mechanisms, 132; and the Oedipus complex, 62, 72, 77, 88. *See also* Puberty; Psychosexual development

Abandonment, fear of, 116

Adler, Alfred, 203

Adrenaline, 109

Adultery, 138–139

Agency, hunger for, 89

Aggression: and defense mechanisms, 124, 132–134; and guilt, 142, 146; and the Oedipus complex, 60–61, 86; and psychosexual development, 42. *See also* Aggressors

Aggressor(s): identification with, 86–87, 132–134; introjection of the, 133. *See also* Aggression

Agoraphobia, 113. *See also* Phobias

Anal period, 38, 44–47. *See also* Psychosexual development

Anger, 16, 22; and defense mechanisms, 134–136; and dreams, 163; and grief, 173–174, 180; and guilt, 137–139; and the Oedipus complex, 55–57; and psychosexual development, 44; and transference, 185

Anorexia, 43–44. *See also* Food

Anthropology, 59, 70–71, 178

Anxiety: castration, 49, 113, 132; and defense mechanisms, 122–124, 126–128, 132–136; and dreams, 157, 161; and the ego, 27; first theory of, 106–107; and guilt, 108–109, 113, 115, 119; and incest, 112–113, 115; involvement of, in our problems, 114–116; and love, 111, 112–113; and neurosis, 114–116; and the Oedipus complex, 115; overview of, 105–120; and panic attacks, 114, 149; reduction of, 116–120; and repression, 105–109, 113; second theory of, 107–113, 136; and sexuality, 106–107, 109, 113, 116, 117; three kinds of, 136; and trauma, 110–12, 116. *See also* Fear

Aron, Lew, 199

Assault on Truth (Masson), 63

Association: and dreams, 158, 159, 163, 166; free, 36, 163; and grief, 172; techniques, 19

Atomic weapons, 126–127

Auto-eroticism, 51. *See also* Sexuality

Baker, John, 175

Baptists, 178

Beethoven, Ludwig von, 130, 196
Behaviorism, 5
Benjamin, Jessica, 3, 61, 65, 66, 88, 89
Bereavement. *See* Grief; Mourning
Bettleheim, Bruno, 134
Beyond the Pleasure Principle (Freud), 98, 101, 102
Biology, 39, 140
Birth: and anxiety, 110–111; control, 107
Bisexuality, 76. *See also* Homosexuality
Breuer, Joseph, 181, 182
Bulimia, 43–44. *See also* Food
Burgoine, E., 178, 179

Campbell, Joseph, 7, 203
Carnivores, 110
Castration: anxiety, 49, 113, 132; and defense mechanisms, 132; and the Oedipus complex, 68, 71, 86, 87
Cathexis, 40
Censorship, 19, 157, 158–163, 204
Chodorow, Nancy, 3, 65
Cigarette smoking, 126, 127–128
Civilization and Its Discontents (Freud), 2, 102, 137, 146, 153
Class, socioeconomic, 59, 60, 80
Cleanliness, compulsive, 46–47
Clitoris, 48
Coitus interruptus, 106–107
Collective unconscious, 169. *See also* Unconscious
Compulsion, repetition, 93–103
Concentration camps, 134
Condensation, and dreams, 159
Conditioning, Pavlovian, 117
Confidentiality, 185
Congitive therapy, 5, 117
Conscience, 24, 26–27; and anxiety, 115, 116; and defense mechanisms, 121; and guilt, 147

Consciousness: and defense mechanisms, 124; as only a small part of mental life, 18–19; pre-, 19–21, 25–26
Constancy principle, 106
Copernicus, 205
Counter-phobia, 132. *See also* Phobias
Countertransference, 197–198. *See also* Transference
Creativity: and the ego, 27; and primary processes, 25

Darwin, Charles, 205
Daydreaming, 21, 156
Death: and anxiety, 114–116; instinct, and repetition compulsion, 102–103. *See also* Grief
Defecation, 44, 45, 47
Defense mechanisms, 27, 204; and aggression, 124, 132–134; definition of, 123; and denial, 126–128; and displacement,134–136; and fantasies, 125, 129–130; and guilt, 121, 124–125, 131, 133–136; and identification with the aggressor, 132–134; and projection, 128–132; and reaction formation, 130–132; and the superego, 121, 124–125, 132–133, 136
Delayed gratification, 23, 27, 98
Delphi, Oracle at, 201
Denial, 126–128
Depression: and grief, 173, 178; and guilt, 149–150
Depth: psychology, 168; therapy, 202–203
Desensitization, 117–120
Development, psychosexual: anal period of, 38, 44–47; and fixation, 39–41; genital period of, 38, 51, 75–79; and infantile sexuality, 41–42; latency period of, 4–5, 38,

51, 73–75; overview of, 35–54; and
regression, 39–41. *See also* Sexuality

Diapers, 47

Diseases, sexually-transmitted, 24, 113

Displacement, 134–136, 159

Divorce, 53, 83–84

"Don Juan" syndrome, 84–85

Dr. Jekyll and Mr. Hyde (Stevenson),
25–26

Dreams, 29–31, 204; and associations,
158, 159, 163, 166; and the ego,
157; interpretation of, current state
of, 167–170; and neurosis, 155,
157–158, 167; and the Oedipus
complex, 155, 167; origin of, 158;
overview of, 155–170; and sexuality,
163–167; symbolism of, 163–167.
See also Daydreams

Drive theory, 5, 37. *See also* Sexuality

Drug addiction, 99–101

Eating disorders, 43–44. *See also*
Food

Ego: and anxiety, 112; basic
description of, 26–27; and defense
mechanisms, 121–124, 126, 128,
134; and dreams, 157; and grief,
175; and guilt, 145; and repetition
compulsion, 98–99; repression in
the service of, 28; strength and
flexibility of, 27–28; and
transference, 186. *See also*
Superego

"Ego and the Id" (Freud), 174

Ego and the Mechanisms of Defense
(Freud), 123

Einstein, Albert, 205

Energy systems, 106–107

Eros, 102. *See also* Love; Sexuality

Erotogenic zones, 48–50. *See also*
Sexuality

European Renaissance, 205

Exile, 115

Fantasies, 191–194, 197; and defense
mechanisms, 125, 129–130; and
dreams, 163; and guilt, 143; and the
Oedipus complex, 57–58, 63; and
psychosexual development, 35,
36–37, 51; and transference, 186

Fasting, practice of, 178

Fear, 12, 16, 142; and defense
mechanisms, 131; and the Oedipus
complex, 57, 61, 69, 84; and
pleasure, 23–24; and primary
processes, 21–22. *See also* Anxiety

Feeding, of babies, 42–43

Feminism, 2–3, 61, 65–66, 68, 89–90

Finger-painting, 46–47

Fixation, 39–41; anal, 46–47; oral,
43–44; phallic, 49–50, 53; and
regression, strong relation between,
52; and repetition compulsion,
93

Flying, fear of, 118

Folktales, 59, 60

Food: and longing for comfort, 22;
need for, 4; and psychosexual
development, 37. *See also* Eating
disorders

Free association, 36, 163. *See also*
Association

Freud, Anna, 123, 125–126, 132–133,
136

Freud, Sigmund (specific works):
Beyond the Pleasure Principle, 98,
101, 102; *Civilization and Its
Discontents*, 2, 102, 137, 146, 153;
"Ego and the Id," 174; *Ego and the
Mechanisms of Defense*, 123;
Interpretation of Dreams, 34, 56–57,
155, 157, 164, 200; *Introductory
Lectures*, 15, 30, 32, 35, 155;
"Mourning and Melancholia,"
171–172, 174, 177; *Psychopathology
of Everyday Life*, 32–33; *Three
Essays on The Theory Sexuality*, 34,

35, 200; *Transference in
Psychotherapy*, 181
*Freud's Concept of Repression and
Defense* (Madison), 121

Gambling, 127
Generalization, stimulus, 29
Genetics, 58
Genital period: basic description of,
38, 51; and the Oedipus complex,
75–79. *See also* Psychosexual
development
Gill, Merton, 168, 191–193
Gorer, G., 178, 179
Gratification, delaying, 23, 27, 98
Grief: and anger, 173–174, 180; and
love, 175–177; overview of,
171–180
Guilt, 12, 27; and anxiety, 108–109,
113, 115, 119; and defense
mechanisms, 121, 124–125, 131,
133–136; and dreams, 156, 157;
noisy, 138–139; and the Oedipus
complex, 57, 69, 72, 74, 81, 84;
overview of, 137–154; and pleasure,
23–24; and psychosexual
development, 48; and repetition
compulsion, 97; and repression,
146, 150; quiet, 138–139; silent, 139,
146; and sin, 144, 146; and the
superego, 26–27, 137–138, 140,
142–143, 145–147; survivor, 10; and
transference, 151–152, 187, 204;
over unconscious wishes, 22–23;

Hallucinations, 182
Harvard College Lecture, 94
Heart rate, 108, 109, 110
Helplessness, anticipation of, 110, 111
Hero With a Thousand Faces, The
(Campbell), 7
Hobbes, Thomas, 140
Hoffman, Irwin, 199

Holocaust, 134
Homosexuality: and defense
mechanisms, 128–129; and the
Oedipus complex, 76, 77–78, 87.
See also Sexuality
Humiliation, 18

Id: and anxiety, 112; basic description
of, 26–27; and defense mechanisms,
121, 124; and repression, 28
Identification: with aggressors, 86–87,
132–134; and guilt, 143
Impotence, 17–18
Incest: and anxiety, 112–113, 115; and
defense mechanisms, 125; and guilt,
143; and the Oedipus complex,
62–63, 69, 79, 84; taboo, 79, 84. *See
also* Sexual abuse
Inferiority, sense of, 50
Inhibition, Symptom, and Anxiety
(Freud), 105, 107
Instinct: classification of, 4; death,
102–103; and the id, 26; and the
latency period, 5; and psychosexual
development, 39; and repetition
compulsion, 101–103
Interpretation of Dreams, The (Freud),
34, 56–57, 155, 157, 164, 200
Intersubjectivity, 198–200
Introductory Lectures (Freud), 15, 30,
32, 35, 155

Jealousy: and defense mechanisms,
134–136; and the Oedipus
complex, 55–57
Johnson, Allen W., 59, 61
Joyce, James, 50
Jung, C. G., 167, 169–170, 203

Kohut, Heinz, 62, 168, 193–196

Latency period: basic description of,
4–5, 38, 51; and the Oedipus

complex, 73–75. *See also* Psychosexual development

Lear, Jonathan, 1, 7–8

Leviathan, The (Hobbes), 140

Library of Congress, 4

Lindemann, Erich, 177, 180

Lindzey, Gardner, 58

Lippman, Paul, 167–169

Loneliness: and eating disorders, 43–44; and grief, 179

Love, 21–22, 79–80: and defense mechanisms, 125, 127, 134–136; and guilt, 141–142; and grief, 175–177; loss of, danger of, 112, 141–142; and the Oedipus complex, 74–76, 78, 88; and repetition compulsion, 95–96; and transference, 190, 194–195

Machiavelli, N., 205

McWilliams, Nancy, 133

Madison, Peter, 121

"Madonna-and-the-whore" phenomenon, 79

Mahler, Margaret, 66–67

Marriage, 13, 15, 17–18, 61

Marx, Karl, 205

Masson, Jeffery, 63

Masturbation, 24, 48–50; and dreams, 167; and the Oedipus complex, 74. 82–83; and regression, 52. *See also* Sexuality

Memory: and grief, 172; and repetition compulsion, 98–99; repressed, 98–99

Mind, three systems composing, 25–26

Mitchell, Stephen, 199

Mourning, 171–180

"Mourning and Melancholia" (Freud), 171–172, 174, 177

Mozart, W. A., 165, 196

Narcotics Anonymous, 100

Nazi concentration camps, 134

Negative transference, 184–185. *See also* Transference

Neurosis: and anxiety, 112, 114–116; basic description of, 157; and defense mechanisms, 122, 125–126; and dreams, 155, 157–158, 167; and the ego, 27; and the Oedipus complex, 62–63; and repetition compulsion, 98; and sexuality, 4, 201–202; symptoms of, 31–32; and transference, 188–189, 198–199

Noisy guilt, 138–139. *See also* Guilt

Nuclear weapons, 126–127

Object relations theory, 5, 37, 39

Oedipus complex, 34, 38, 200, 204; and anxiety, 115; consequences of, 84–91; and defense mechanisms, 132, 133, 136; and dreams, 155, 167; and guilt, 57, 69, 72, 74, 81, 84, 143; and incest, 62–63, 69, 79, 84; and "the Oedipal victor," 80–84; overview of, 55–91; and passivity, 64, 89; and rapproachement conflict, 66–67; and repetition compulsion, 93; resolution of, 69, 72–73, 75–79, 86–87; and the tenderness/passion split, 79–80; three major implications of, 64; and transference, 188–190, 194–195; universality of, 49. *See also* Psychosexual development

Oedipus Rex (Sophocles), 55–57

Oedipus Ubiquitous (Price-Williams), 49

Opened Minded (Lear), 7–8

Opera, 165–166

Oracle at Delphi, 201

Oral period, 38, 42–44. *See also* Psychosexual development

Oral sex, 44
Organizing principles, 9
Orgasm, sex without, 106–107

Panic attacks, 114, 149. *See also* Anxiety
Pappenheim, Bertha, 181, 182
Paranoia, 129, 130
Parapraxes, 29, 32–34
Parental responses: to defecation, 45; to the oral period, 42–43
Parkes, Colin Murray, 178, 179
Passivity, 50, 64, 88–89
Patricide, 69, 115. *See also* Oedipus complex
Pavlovian conditioning, 117
Penis, 48–50; and dreams, 164, 166; and the Oedipus complex, 68–69, 71, 88. *See also* Phallic period
Perceptual-conscious, 25–26
Perversion, 36
Phallic period: basic description of, 38, 47–50; and the Oedipus complex, 73. *See also* Penis; Psychosexual development
Phobia: agora-, 113; and anxiety, 117–119; counter-, 132; treatment of, 117–119
Pleasure: and anxiety, 111; and guilt, 140, 141, 142, 146; principle, 23–25, 98, 99, 101–102; and repetition compulsion, 98, 99, 101–102
Political views, 22
Polygamous cultures, 70–71
Polymorphous perversion, 36
Pornography, 52–53
Portrait of the Artist as a Young Man (Joyce), 50
Positive transference, 184, 185. *See also* Transference
Prayer, 178. *See also* Religion
Preconsciousness, 19–21, 25–26
Pregnancy, 77, 110, 182

Price-Williams, Douglass, 59–60, 61
Primary process: basic description of, 21–25; and the ego, 27–28; and guilt, 143, 145–146; and the Oedipus complex, 63
Primates, 110
Processes: primary, 21–25, 27–28, 63, 143, 145–146; secondary, 21–22, 25–26
Projection, as a defense mechanism, 128–133
Psychoanalytic training institutes, 6
Psychopathology of Everyday Life (Freud) 32–33
Psychosexual development: anal period of, 38, 44–47; and fixation, 39–41; genital period of, 38, 51, 75–79; and infantile sexuality, 41–42; latency period of, 4–5, 38, 51, 73–75; overview of, 35–54; and regression, 39–41
Puberty, 38, 73–75. *See also* Adolescence; Psychosexual development
Punishment: and anxiety, 115; and defense mechanisms, 121; and dreams, 161; and guilt, 140–144, 146; and transference, 187

Quiet guilt, 138–139. *See also* Guilt

Rapproachement conflict, 66–67
Reaction formation, 130–132
Reality: laws of, 21; principle, 23–26, 98; and repetition compulsion, 98; testing, 126
Rebelliousness, 22, 47
Reconciliation, 67
Regression: and the ego, 28; and fixation, 58; and masturbation, 52; and psychosexual development, 39–41, 51–54
Relational therapy, 168

Relaxation: and anxiety, 117–118; progressive, 118

Religion: and grief, 178; and guilt, 144–145, 146

Remorse, 143

Repetition compulsion, 93–103

Replay transference, 195–197. *See also* Transference

Repression, 146, 150; anxiety, 105–109, 113; basic description of, 18–19; and defense mechanisms, 122–126, 128–132; and dreams, 157; and the ego, 27; and the id, 28; and the Oedipus complex, 63, 73, 74; and repetition compulsion, 98–99; and the three systems composing the human mind, 26; too much, costs of, 28–29

Resistance, 18–19

Resolution, of the Oedipus complex, 69, 72–73, 75–79, 86–87

Ritual, 178

Sadism, 44, 47

Saint Francis, 144–145

Sainthood, 144–146

Salome, Lou Andreas, 45

Schwaber, E. A., 181

Scotland, 179

Secondary process, 21–22, 25–26

Seduction, 63, 72

Self: and defense mechanisms, 134–136; -destructive behavior, 31–32; -preservation, 4; turning against the, 134–136. *See also* Selfobject

Selfobject: transference, 193–197; use of the term, 194

Sex therapists, 13

Sexual abuse, 62–63, 81–82. *See also* Incest

Sexuality: and anxiety, 106–107, 109, 113, 116, 117; and coitus interruptus, 106–107; and defense mechanisms, 123–126, 128–133; and dreams, 163–167; and drive theory, 5, 37; and grief, 171–172, 175; and the id, 26; and the latency period, 4–5, 38, 51, 73–75; and masturbation, 24, 48–50, 52, 74, 82–83, 167; and neurosis, 31–32, 202–201; and the Oedipus complex, 55–91; and the pleasure principle, 24; and the reality principle, 24–25; and repetition compulsion, 93–103; and transference, 185–187, 188–190, 200. *See also* Psychosexual development; Sexual abuse; Sexually-transmitted diseases

Sexually-transmitted diseases, 24, 113. *See also* Sexuality

Shakespeare, William, 7, 55–56, 70, 90–91, 205

Silent guilt, 139, 146. *See also* Guilt

Sin: and guilt, 144, 146; and transference, 187

Skinner, B. F., 93

Smoking, 126, 127–128

Socialization, 60

Sodium pentothal, 19

Solomon, Maynard, 130

Sophocles, 7, 55–57

Spiritual Baptists, 178

Spirituality. *See* Religion

Stevenson, Robert Louis, 25

Stimulus generalization, 29

Stolorow, Robert, 9–10, 195, 199

Strachey, James, 34, 40, 200

Stress, 43–44. *See also* Anxiety; Fear

Superego: and anxiety, 109, 112, 115; attacks, 109; basic description of, 26–27; and defense mechanisms, 121, 124–125, 132–133, 136; and dreams, 161; and guilt, 137–138, 140, 142–143, 145–147. *See also* Ego

Survivor guilt, 10. *See also* Guilt

Swazi culture, 179

Symbolism, of dreams, 163–167

"Symptamatology and Management of Acute Grief" (Lindemann), 177

Symptom(s): and anxiety, 117–119; and dreams, 157, 158; as representative of unconscious motivations, 11–12; -substitution, 118; and transference, 182

Systematic desensitization, 117–120

Taboo, 58, 79, 84

Template, use of the term, 183

Tenderness: and defense mechanisms, 125; /passion split, 79–80

Three Essays on The Theory Sexuality (Freud), 34, 35, 200

Toilet training, 45

Training institutes, 6

Transference: analysis, contemporary, 191–193; categories of, 184–185; counter-, 197–198; in everyday life, 196–197; and guilt, 151–152; and intersubjectivity, 198–200; negative, 184–185; and neurosis, 188–189, 198–199; positive, 184, 185; replay, 195–197; selfobject, 193–197; and sexuality, 185–187, 188–190; un-neutralized erotic, 185–190

Transference in Psychotherapy, The (Freud), 181

Trauma: and anxiety, 110–112, 116; and birth, 110–111; and defense mechanisms, 136; and transference, 183

Unconscious: collective, 169; and defense mechanisms, 124–125; and depth therapy, 202–203; and dreams, 29–31, 156, 158, 161–162, 167–170; early development of, 5; and guilt, 146,150; and neurotic symptoms, 31–32; and organizing principles, 9; overview of, 15–34; and parapraxes, 29, 32–34; and psychosexual development, 36; and repetition compulsion, 95–96; strange connections that are made in, 13–14; and transference, 199–200; use of the term, 8

Un-neutralized erotic transference, 185–190. *See also* Transference

Unpleasure, use of the term, 97

Venereal disease, 24, 113

Vienna Medical Society, 2

West Indies, 178

Whiting, John, 70–71

Wolpe, Joseph, 117, 118, 119

Works, of Sigmund Freud: *Beyond the Pleasure Principle*, 98, 101, 102; *Civilization and Its Discontents*, 2, 102, 137, 146, 153; "Ego and the Id," 174; *Ego and the Mechanisms of Defense*, 123; *Interpretation of Dreams*, 34, 56–57, 155, 157, 164, 200; *Introductory Lectures*, 15, 30, 32, 35, 155; "Mourning and Melancholia," 171–172, 174, 177; *Psychopathology of Everyday Life*, 32–33; *Three Essays on The Theory Sexuality*, 34, 35, 200; *Transference in Psychotherapy*, 181

World War I, 153

World War II, 2